THE UNITED SHAPES OF AMERICA

The United States Congressional District Coloring Book

**Written by
Nilmini Rubin
& Araliya Rubin**

**Illustrated by
Max Rosenbaum**

**Edited by
Lenora Shishido**

Copyright © 2017 by Nilmini Rubin

ISBN: 978-0-9972787-4-3

 Publisher: Mighty Child
Chevy Chase, MD

All rights reserved. No part of this book may be reproduced in any form or by an electronic or mechanical means, including information storage and retrieval systems, without permission in writing from the publisher, except by a reviewer who may quote brief passages in a review.

Requests for permission to make copies of any parts of this book should be emailed to: books@mightychild.net.

To order bulk or autographed copies of this book, visit www.mightychild.net or email: books@mightychild.net.

We would like to thank Ms. Miller,
one of the best third grade teachers ever,
for her dedication and enthusiasm.

The Articles of Confederation

During a hot summer in 1787, a group of men gathered in Philadelphia, Pennsylvania because they thought the United States was disorganized and inefficient. The Articles of Confederation, the rules the United States had been following, were not working well. Instead of rewriting the Articles of Confederation, they decided to write a new Constitution to create a stronger national government for the United States.

The Constitution

The Constitution of the United States establishes the most important laws and rights for people in the United States. The Constitution creates three branches of the United States Government, so each branch "checks and balances" the other branches.

The three branches are:
1) Congress - to write laws;
2) Judiciary - to review laws and figure out when they have been broken; and
3) Executive - to enforce laws so people follow them.

The Senate

The Senate is the upper chamber of the U.S. Congress. Senators are elected for terms of 6 years. This long term gives them time to think through issues so they are considered to have a "deliberative role." There are two Senators for every state. Since there are 50 states, the total number of Senators is 100. District of Columbia does not have a voting Senator or Representative.

House of Representatives

The House of Representatives is the lower chamber of the U.S. Congress. It is sometimes called the "People's House," the place where they can respond quickly to the concerns of the people. Representatives are elected for short terms of 2 years. In the House of Representatives, there are 435 Congressmen or Congresswomen. Each Representative represents a different Congressional district.

The Difference Between The Senate And The House Of Representatives

George Washington tried to explain the difference between the Senate and the House of Representatives to Thomas Jefferson, who was in Paris, France when the Constitution was written. Washington reportedly said "the Senate is to 'cool' House legislation, just as a saucer was used to cool hot tea."

The Census Determines The Number Of Representatives

The more people in a state, the more Representatives it gets. To figure out exactly how many people each state has, the second section of the Constitution requires that the U.S. count the number of people it has every 10 years. That count is called the census.

Electoral College

Every four years, people at least 18 years old may vote for their pick for President and Vice President. However, they don't directly vote for their picks, they actually vote for electors from their state. Those 538 state electors then vote for President and Vice President.

This process is called the Electoral College. It was established in the Constitution as a compromise between electing the President by a vote in Congress and electing the President by a popular vote. Each state gets the same number of electors as they have in their congressional delegation: one for each member of the House of Representatives, plus one for each Senator. Though the District of Columbia doesn't have a voting congressional delegation, they get 3 electors because of a change made through the 23rd amendment of the Constitution.

Congressional District Lines

Sometimes the congressional districts are drawn with straight lines, sometimes districts are drawn with squiggly lines and sometimes the districts are splotches. For most states, those congressional district lines are drawn directly by the legislatures of the state. The majority of state legislatures are called "bi-cameral" because they are made up of a state-level House of Representatives and a Senate. However, Nebraska is called "unicameral" because it just has a Senate.

There are some states that have groups of people called commissions that advise state legislatures on how to draw the district lines. In a few states, there are independent commissions that actually draw the district lines themselves.

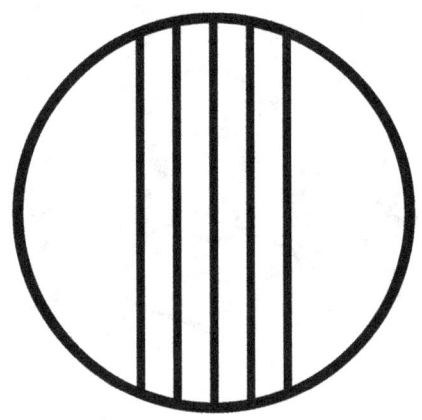
Straight Lines

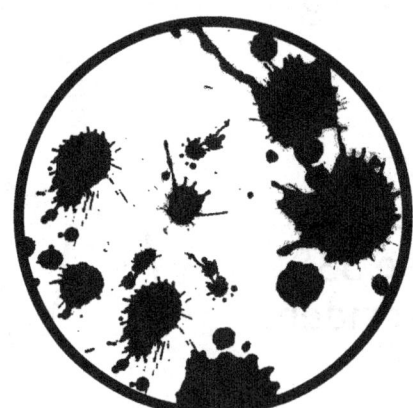
Splotches

Squiggly Lines

Gerrymandering

The word "gerrymandering" was first used in 1812. That year, a bill was passed by the Massachusetts legislature to change the district lines, so one political party had a better chance of winning in the next Massachusetts elections. Even though Governor Elbridge Gerry was not happy about the law changing the district lines, he signed it anyway.

One person thought the new district lines looked like an amphibian and exclaimed "Salamander! Call it a Gerrymander."

Governor Elbridge Gerry

A cartoon map showing an animal around the districts first appeared in the Boston Gazette on March 26, 1812.

Sometimes, people argue that certain congressional districts are "gerrymandered" – that the state was divided to give one political party an electoral majority in as many districts as possible, while concentrating the voting power of the opposing party in a small number of districts.

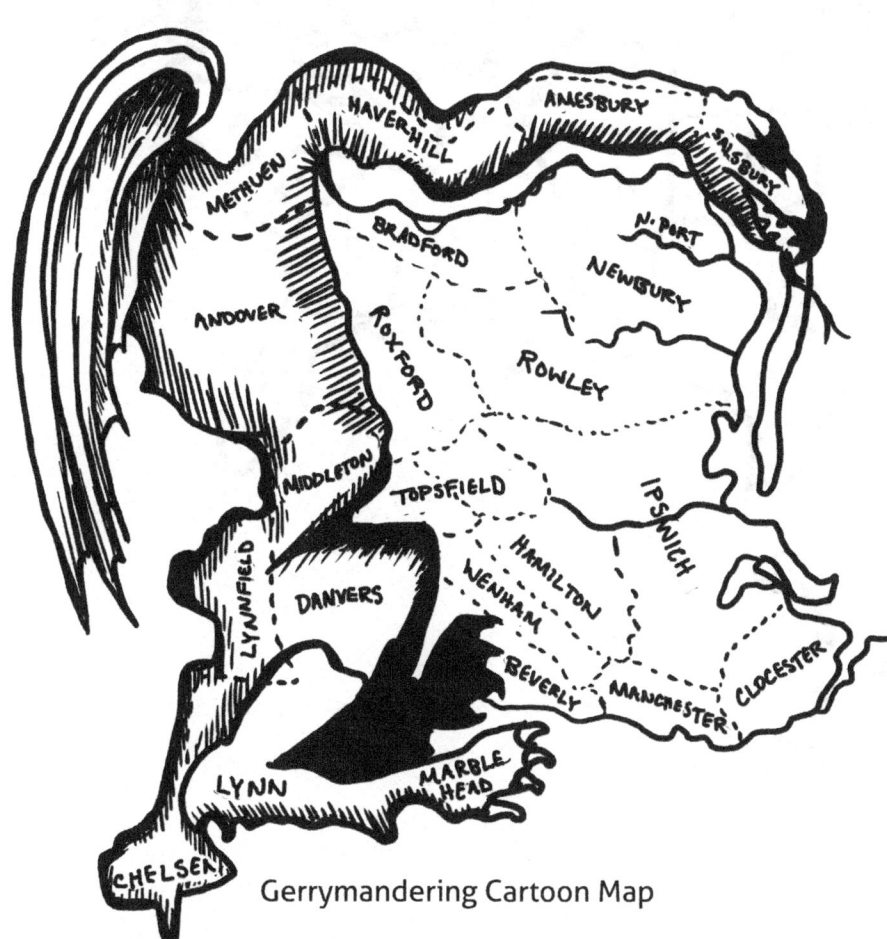

Gerrymandering Cartoon Map

The United States Shapes of America allows you to feel and see each congressional district for yourself. Enjoy!

Congressional Districts by State

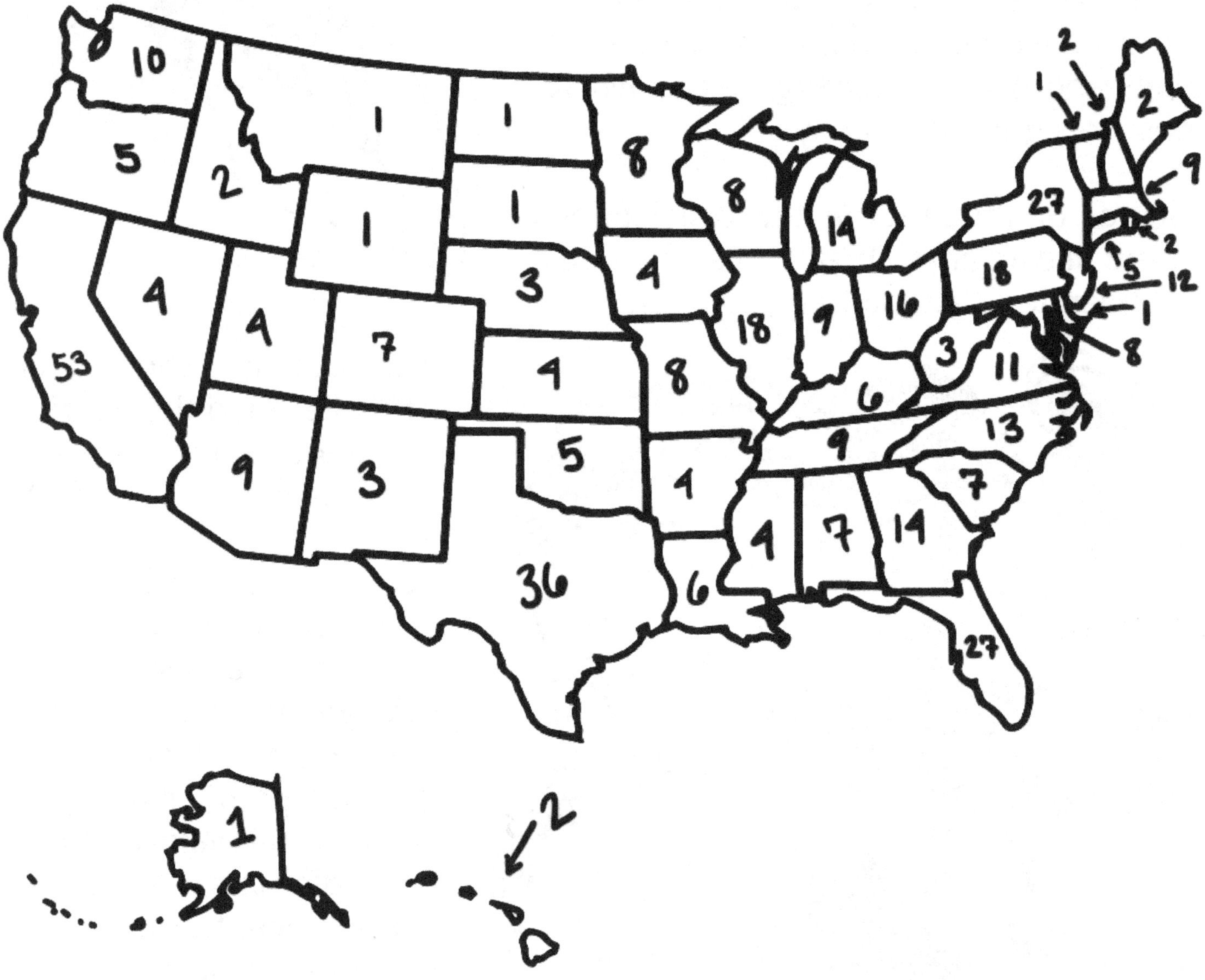

Number of Representatives by State

State	#	State	#
Alabama	7	Nebraska	3
Alaska	1	Nevada	4
Arizona	9	New Hampshire	2
Arkansas	4	New Jersey	12
California	53	New Mexico	3
Colorado	7	New York	27
Connecticut	5	North Carolina	13
Delaware	1	North Dakota	1
Florida	27	Ohio	16
Georgia	14	Oklahoma	5
Hawaii	2	Oregon	5
Idaho	2	Pennsylvania	18
Illinois	18	Rhode Island	2
Indiana	9	South Carolina	7
Iowa	4	South Dakota	1
Kansas	4	Tennessee	9
Kentucky	6	Texas	36
Louisiana	6	Utah	4
Maine	2	Vermont	1
Maryland	8	Virginia	11
Massachusetts	9	Washington	10
Michigan	14	West Virginia	3
Minnesota	8	Wisconsin	8
Mississippi	4	Wyoming	1
Missouri	8		
Montana	1		

ALABAMA

Population: 4.8 million
Representatives: 7

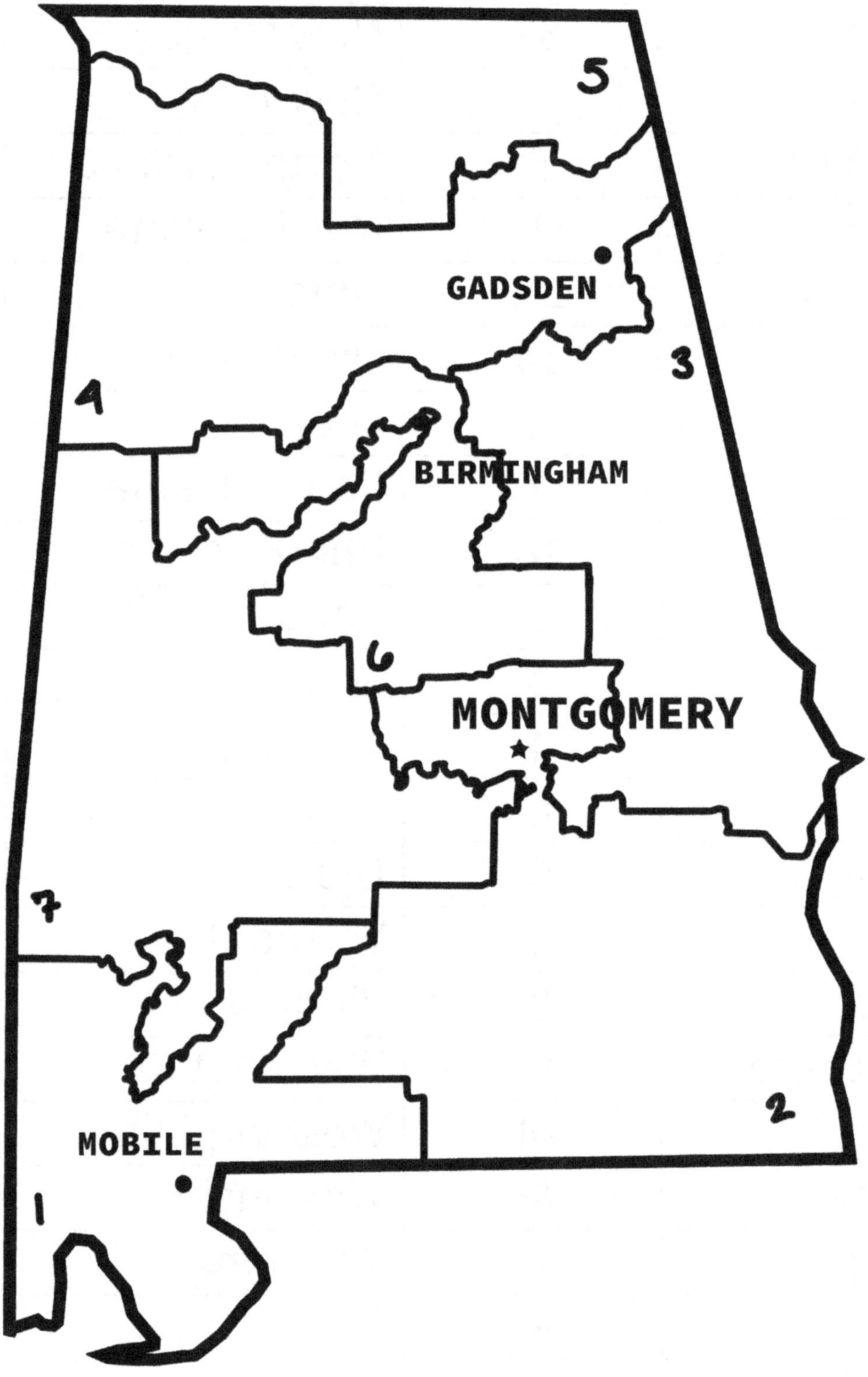

ALASKA

Population: 0.7 million
Representatives: 1

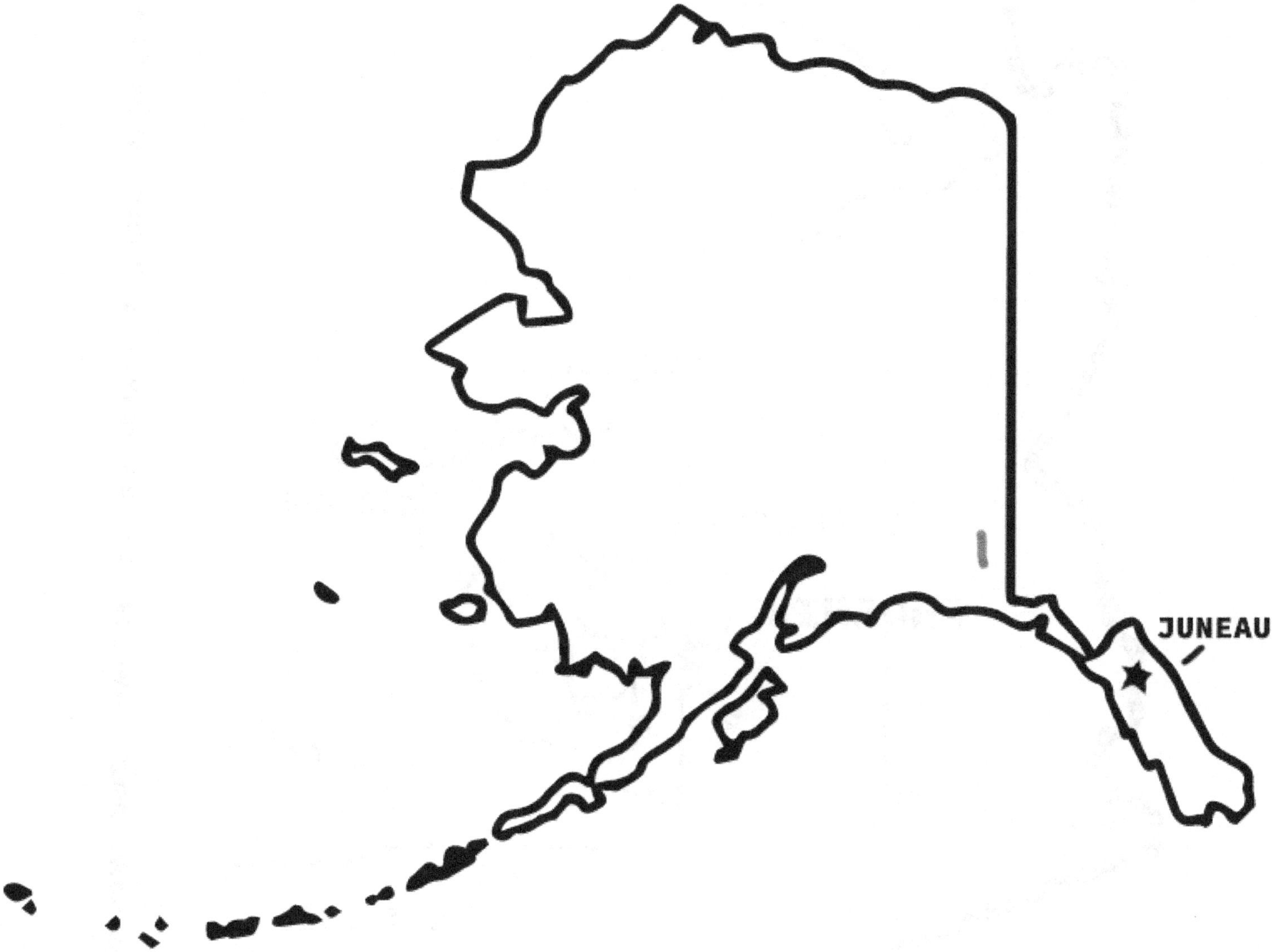

★ JUNEAU

ARIZONA

Population: 6.7 million
Representatives: 9

ARKANSAS

Population: 2.9 million
Representatives: 4

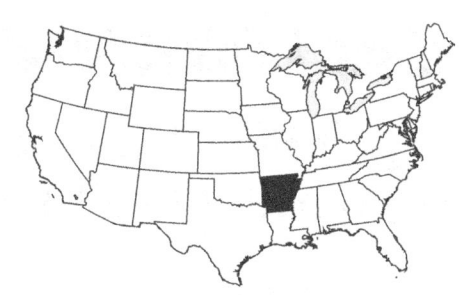

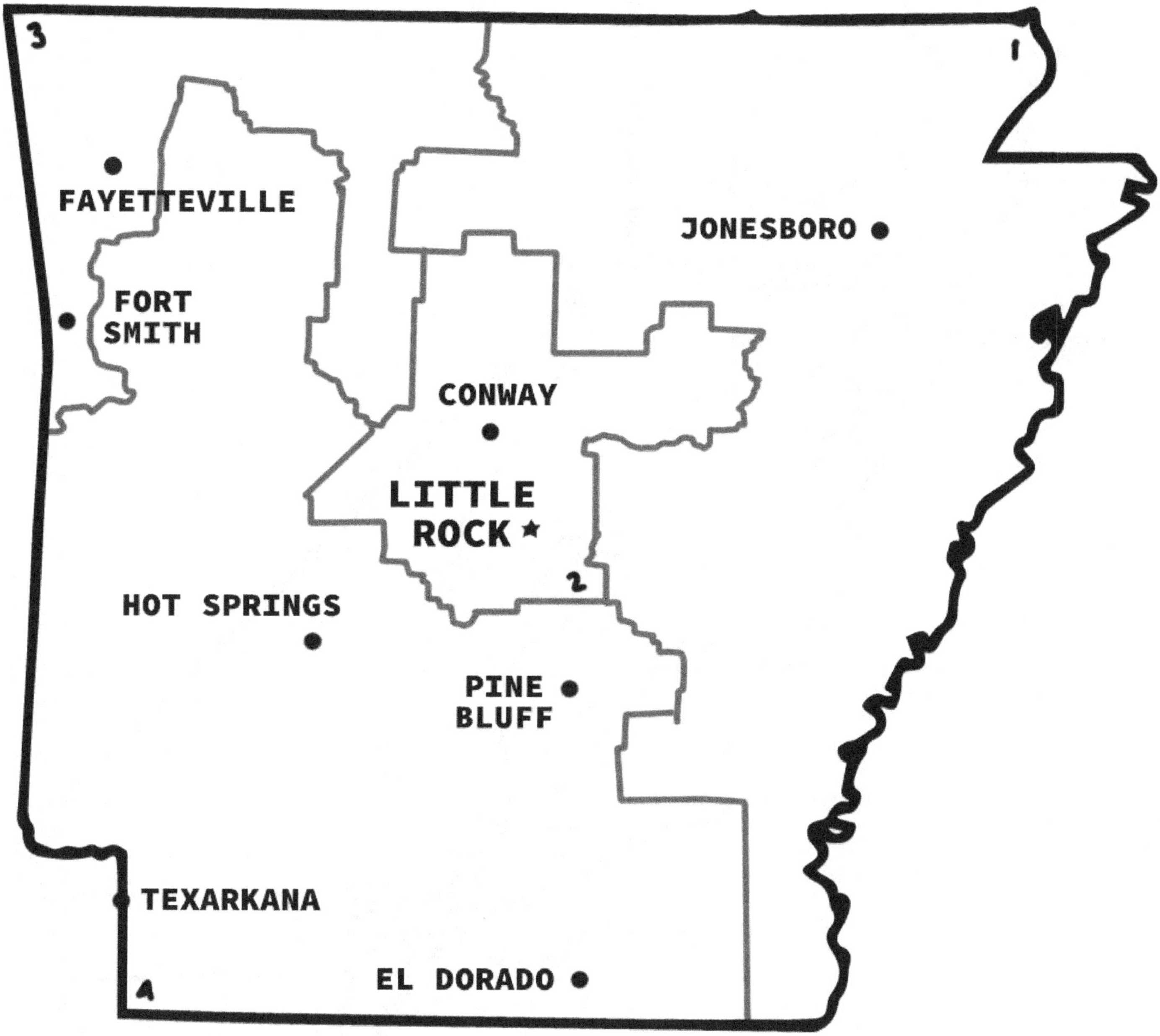
3
1
FAYETTEVILLE
JONESBORO
FORT SMITH
CONWAY
LITTLE ROCK
2
HOT SPRINGS
PINE BLUFF
TEXARKANA
4
EL DORADO

CALIFORNIA

Population: 39.1 million
Representatives: 53

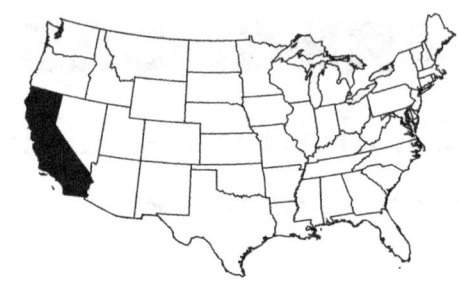

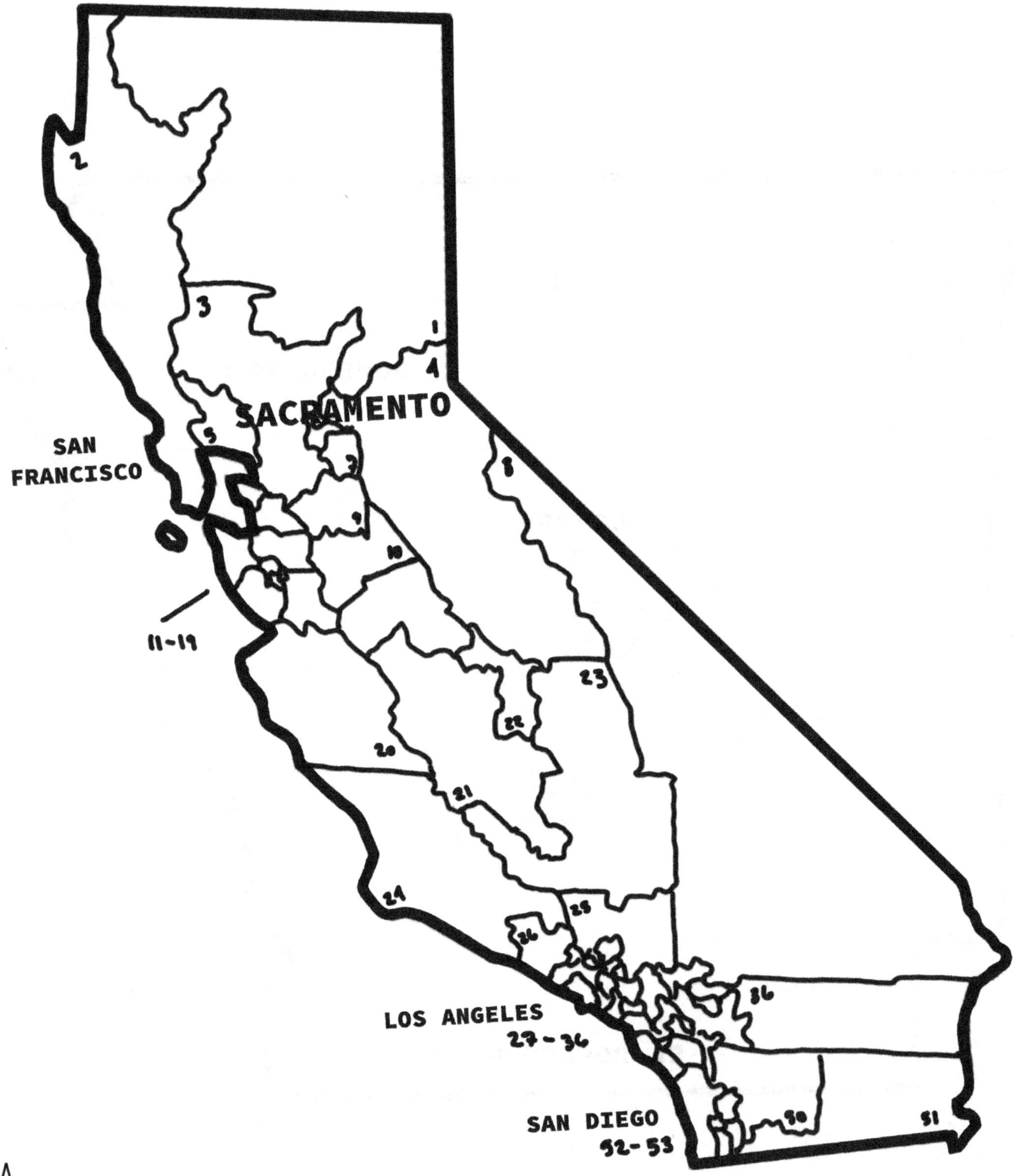
2
3
1
4
SACRAMENTO
5
7
8
9
10
SAN FRANCISCO
11-19
23
22
20
21
24
25
26
LOS ANGELES
27-36
36
SAN DIEGO
52-53
50
51

COLORADO

Population: 5.4 million
Representatives: 7

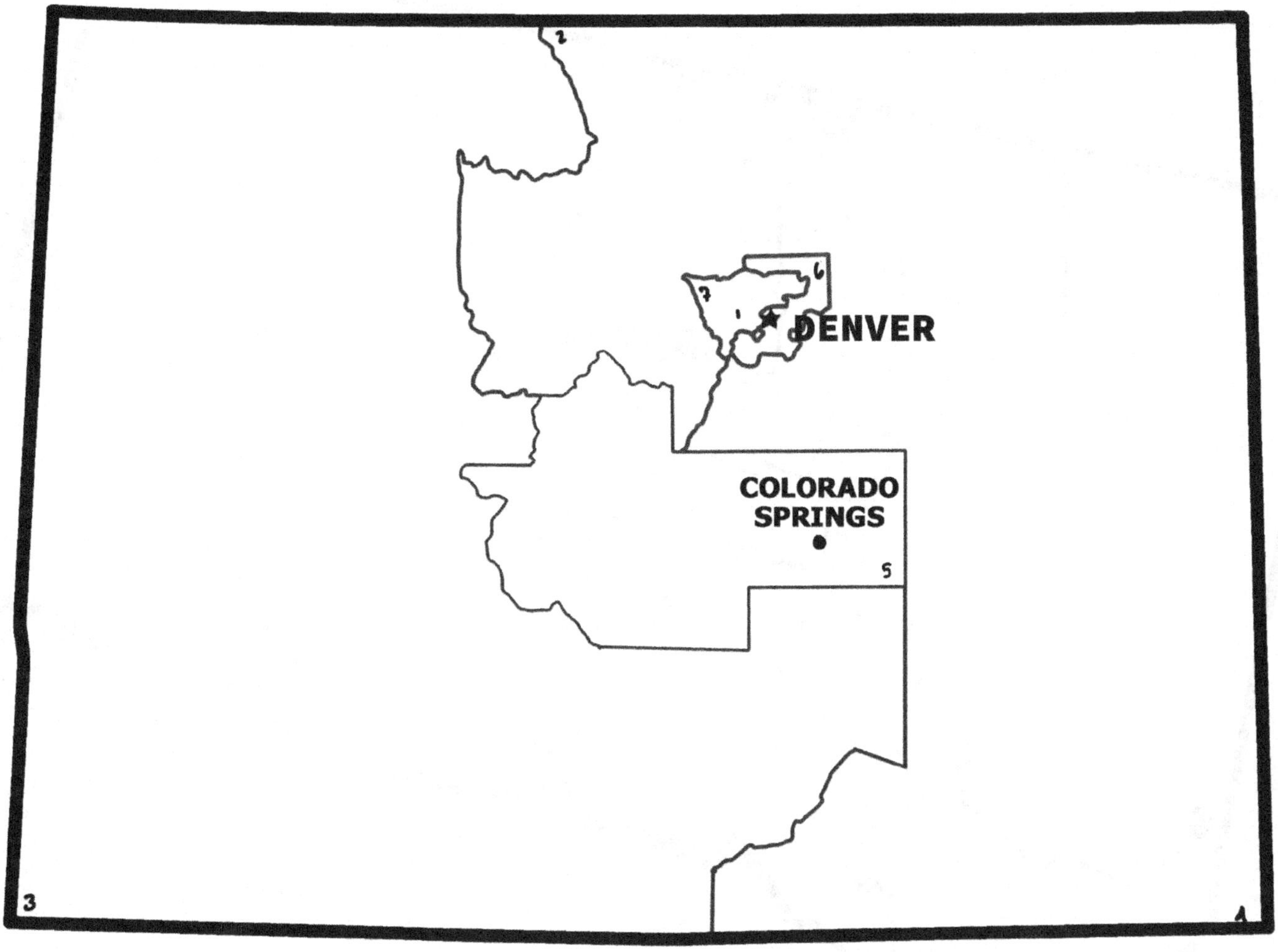

CONNECTICUT

Population: 3.5 million
Representatives: 5

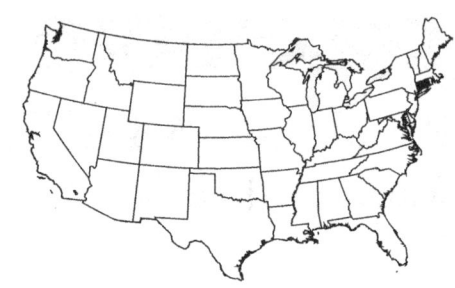

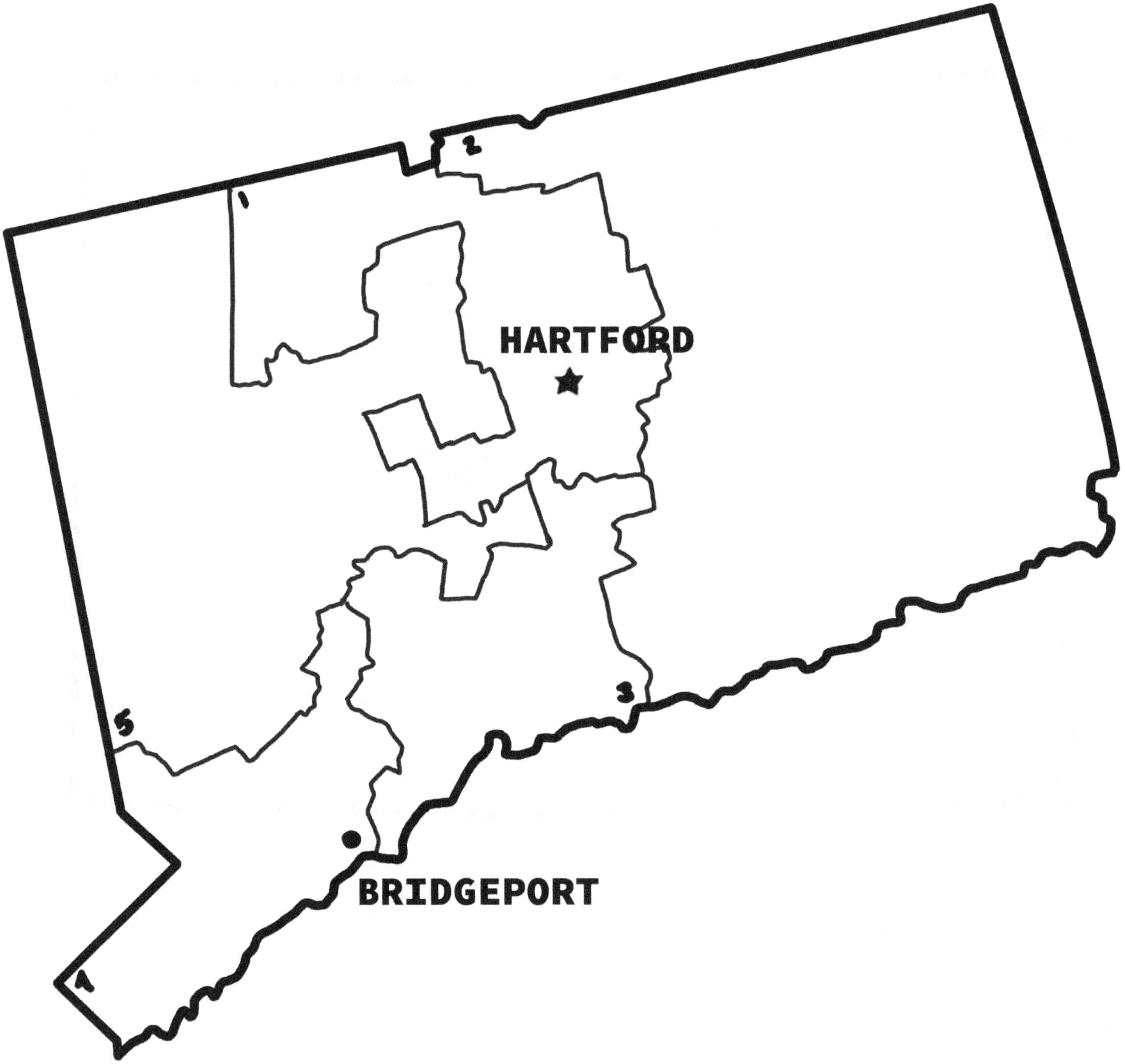
HARTFORD
BRIDGEPORT
1
2
3
4
5

DELAWARE

Population: 0.9 million
Representatives: 1

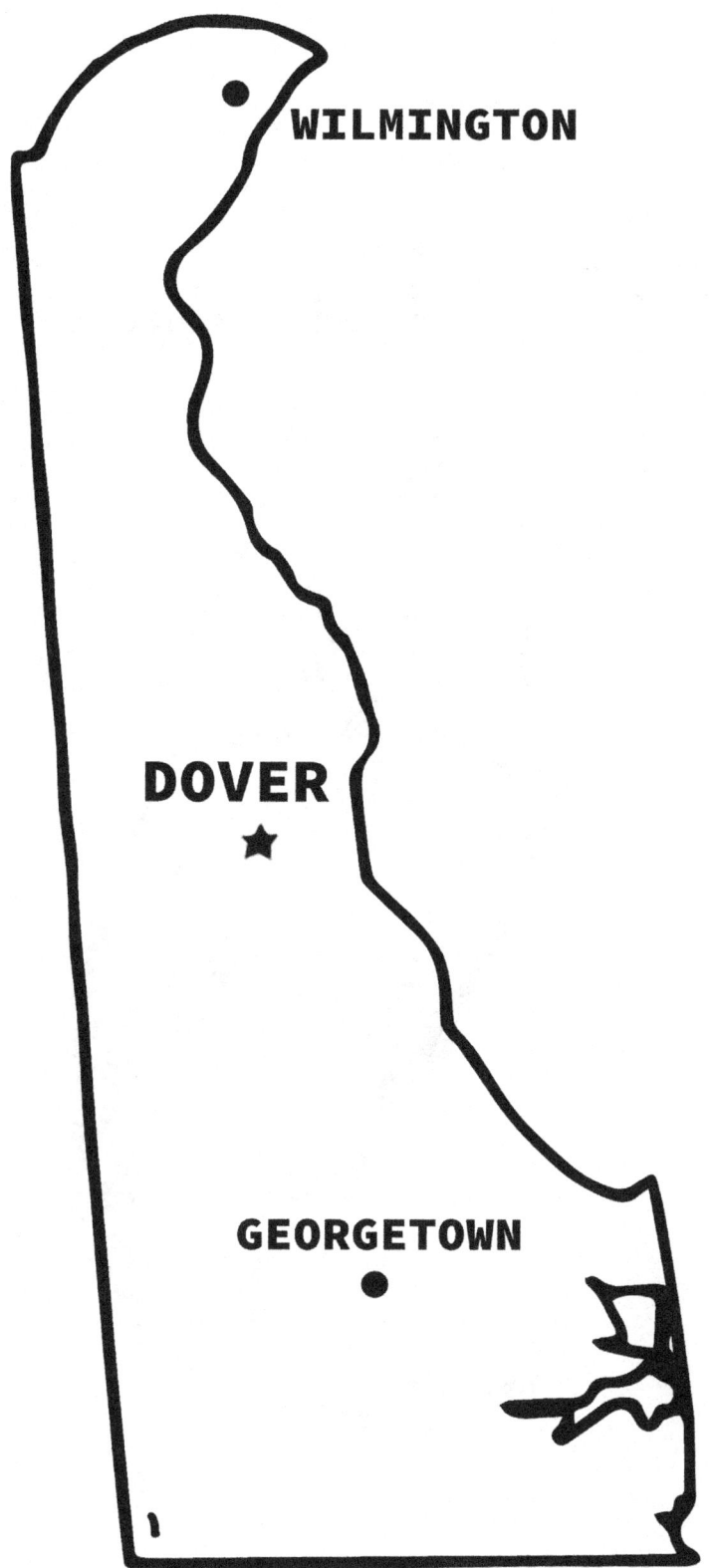

FLORIDA

Population: 20.2 million
Representatives: 27

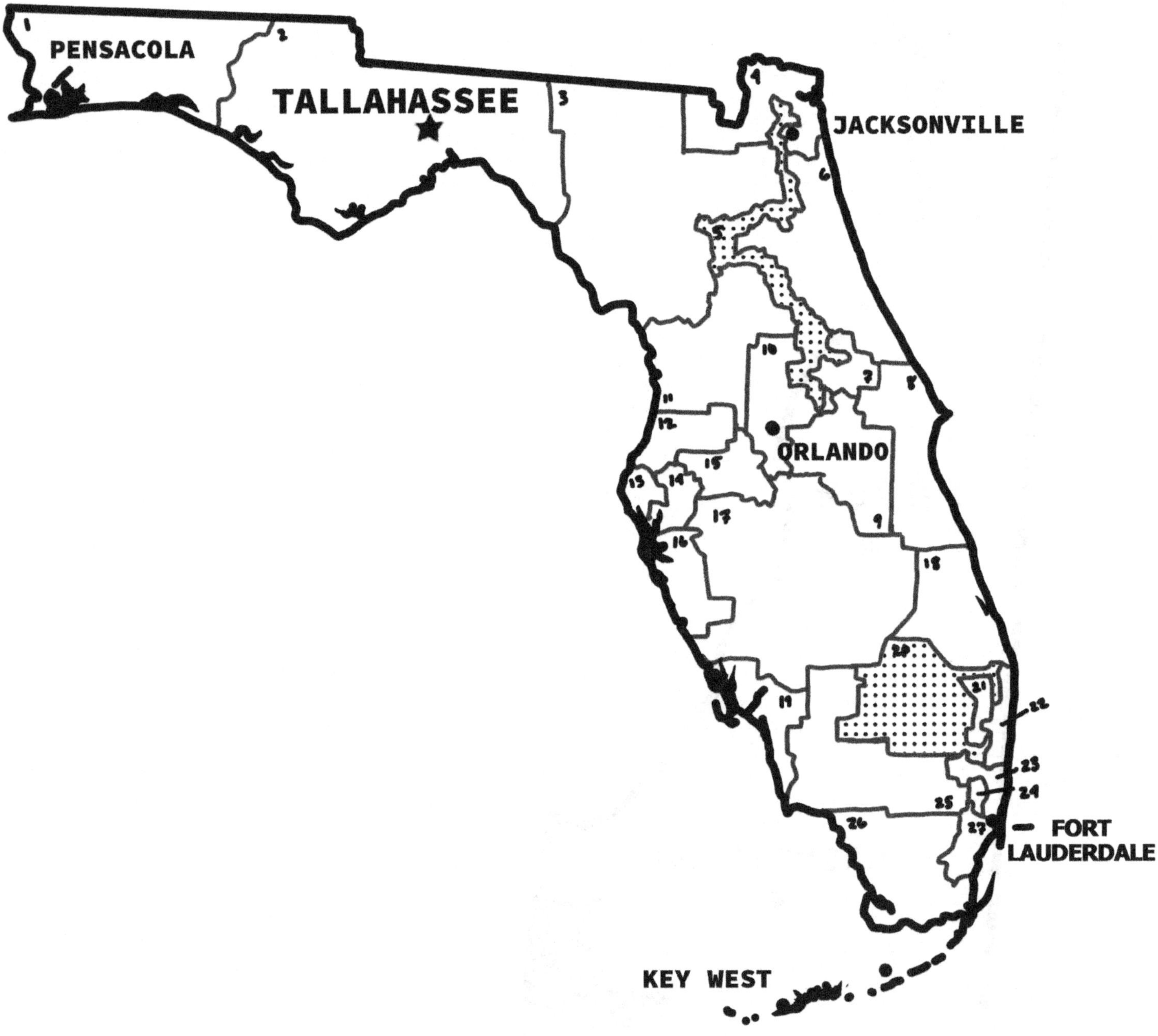

GEORGIA

Population: 10.2 million
Representatives: 14

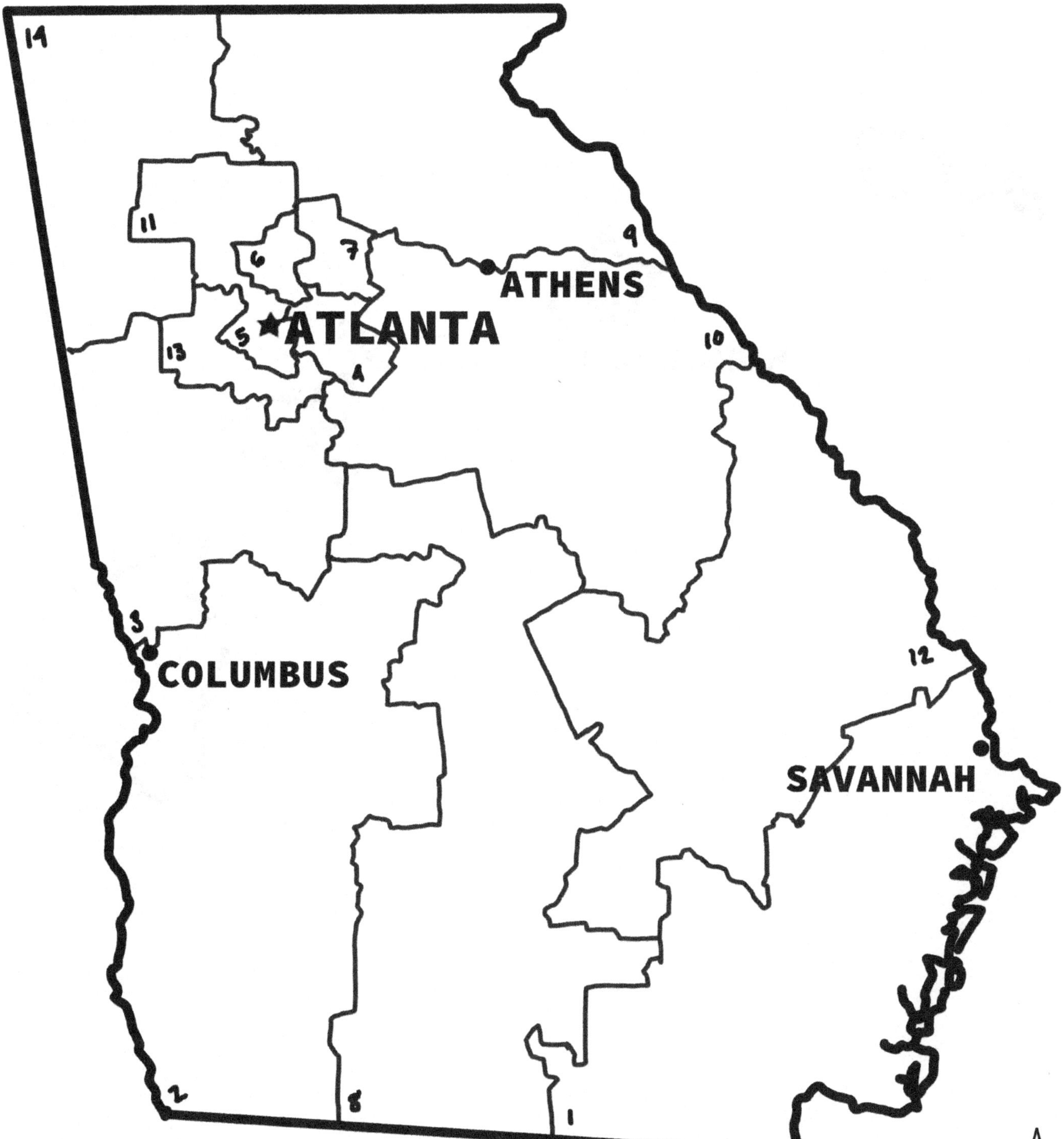

21

HAWAII

Population: 1.4 million
Representatives: 2

HONOLULU

IDAHO

Population: 1.6 million
Representatives: 2

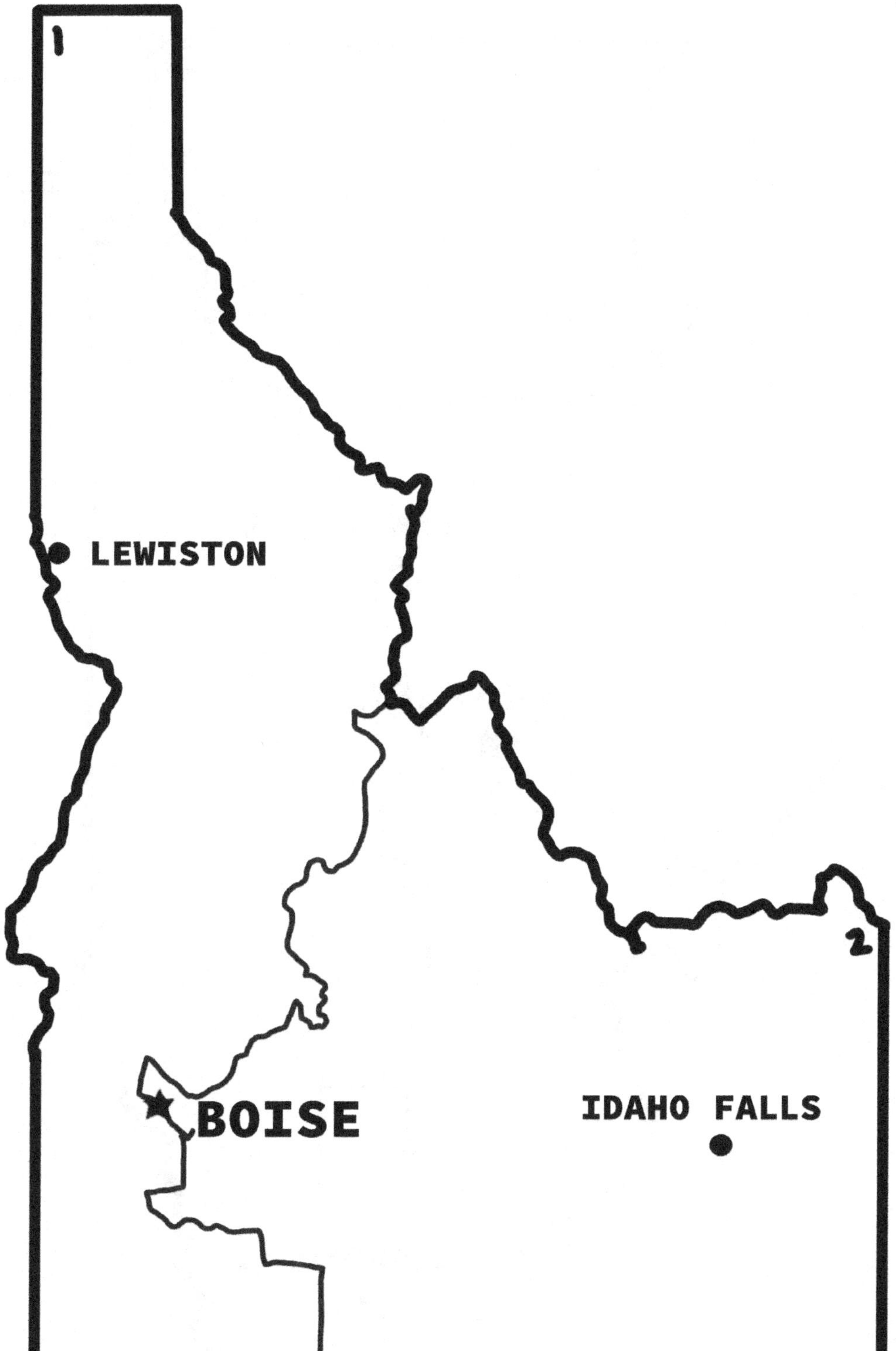

1

● LEWISTON

2

★ BOISE   IDAHO FALLS ●

ILLINOIS

Population: 12.8 million
Representatives: 18

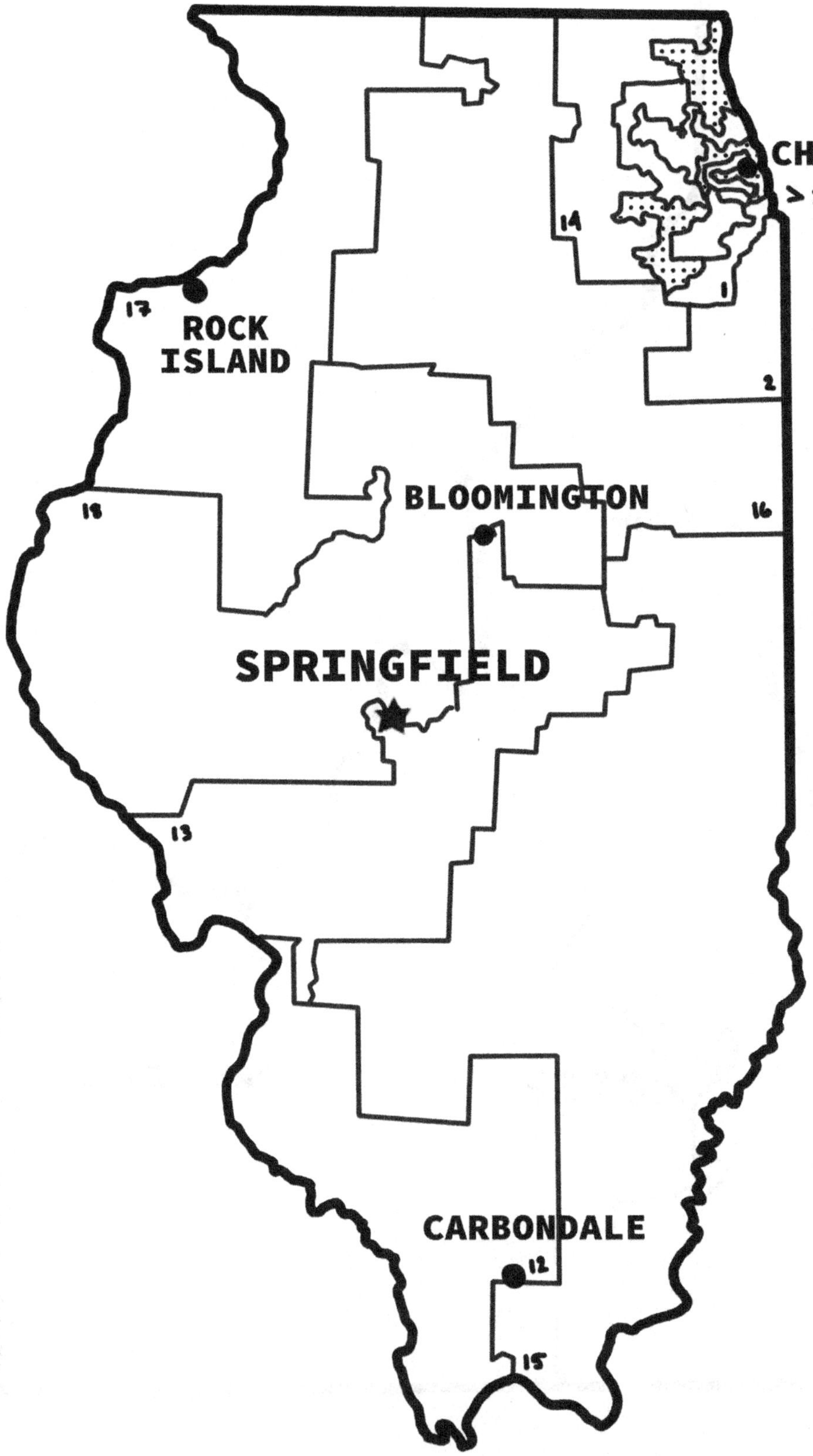

INDIANA

Population: 6.6 million
Representatives: 9

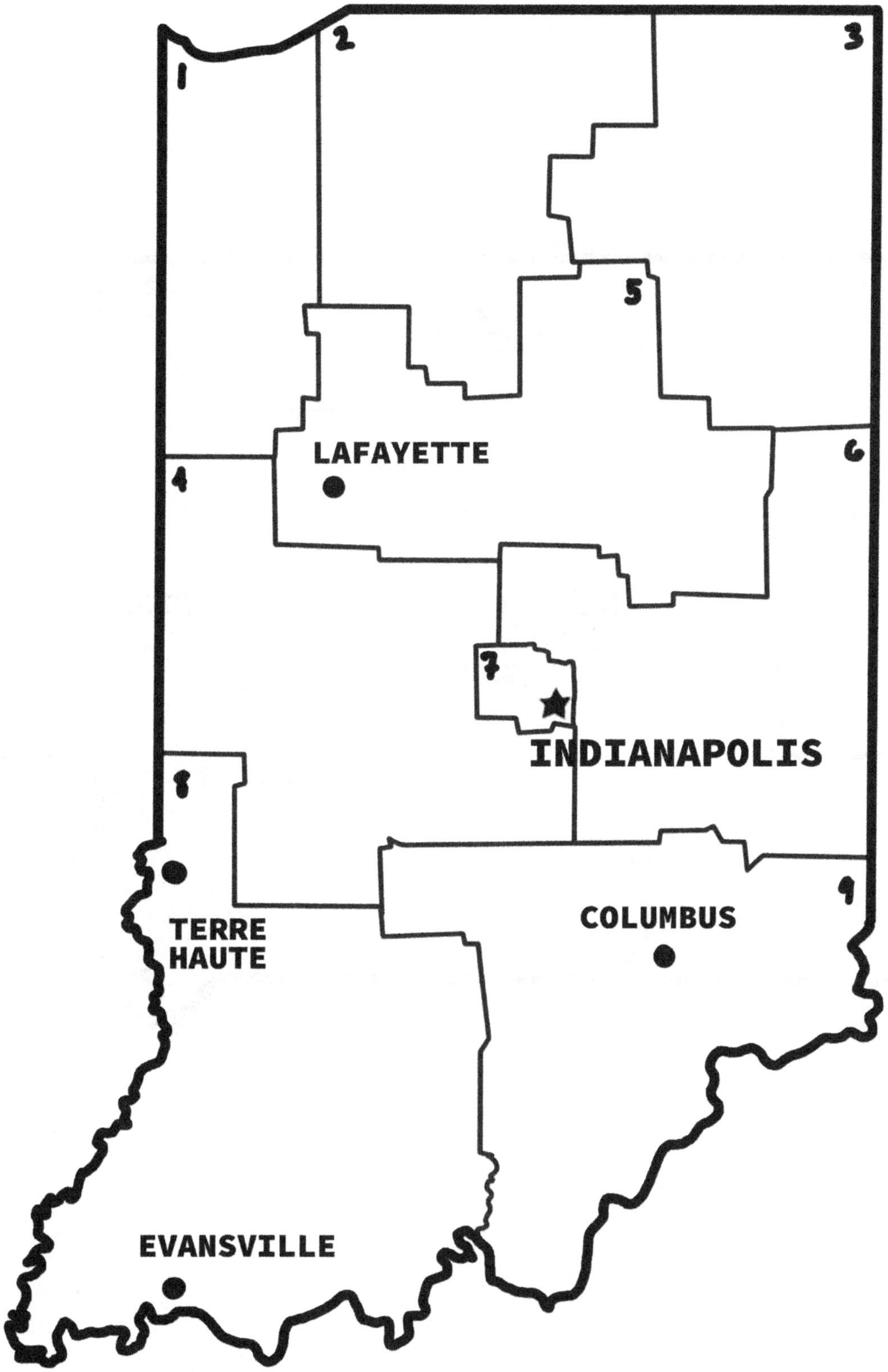

IOWA

Population: 3.1 million
Representatives: 4

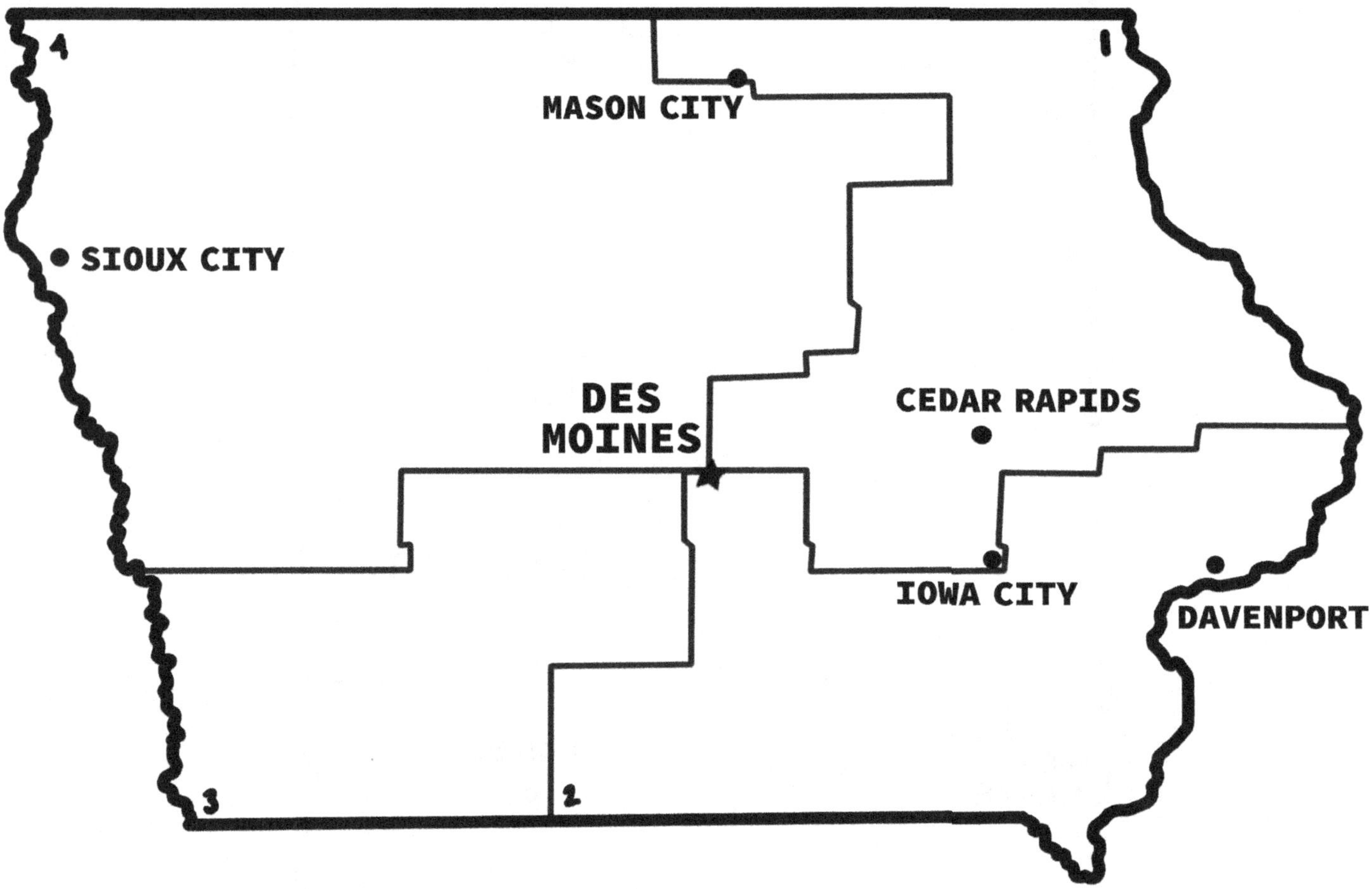

KANSAS

Population: 2.9 million
Representatives: 4

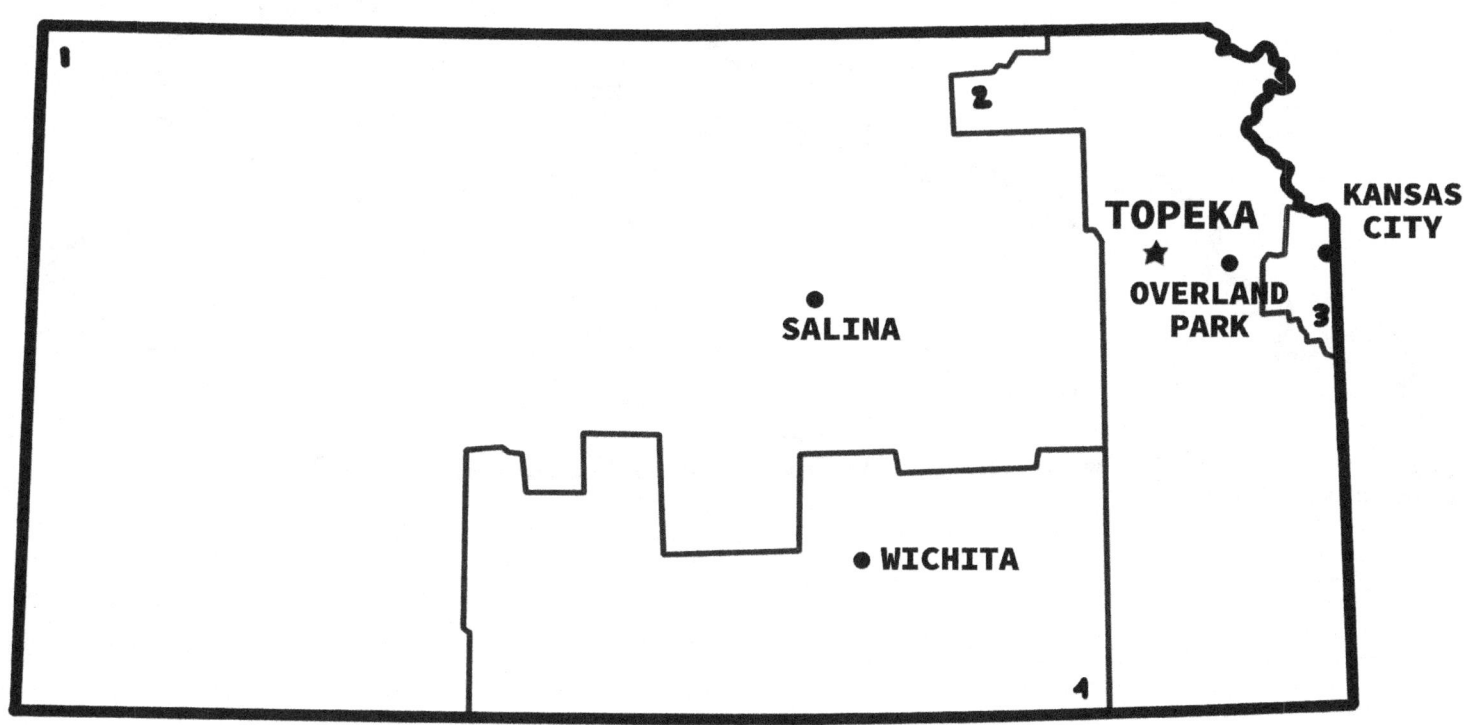

KENTUCKY

Population: 4.4 million
Representatives: 6

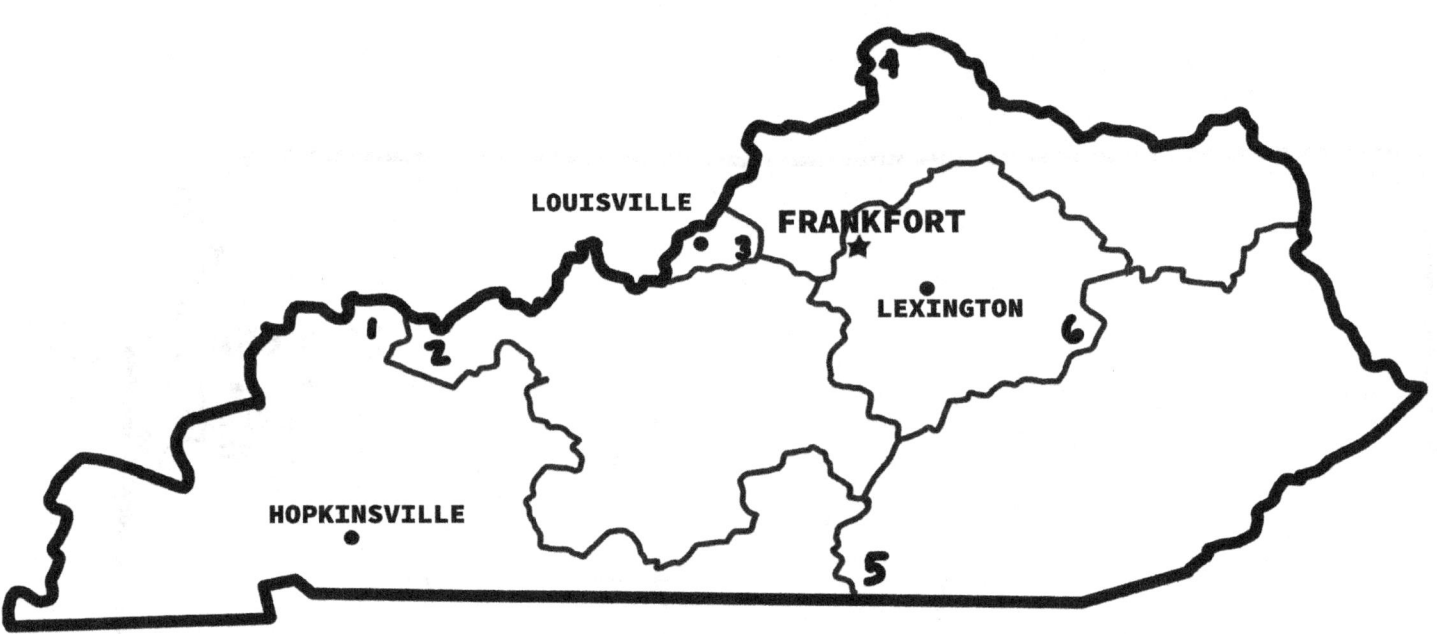

LOUISIANA

Population: 4.6 million
Representatives: 6

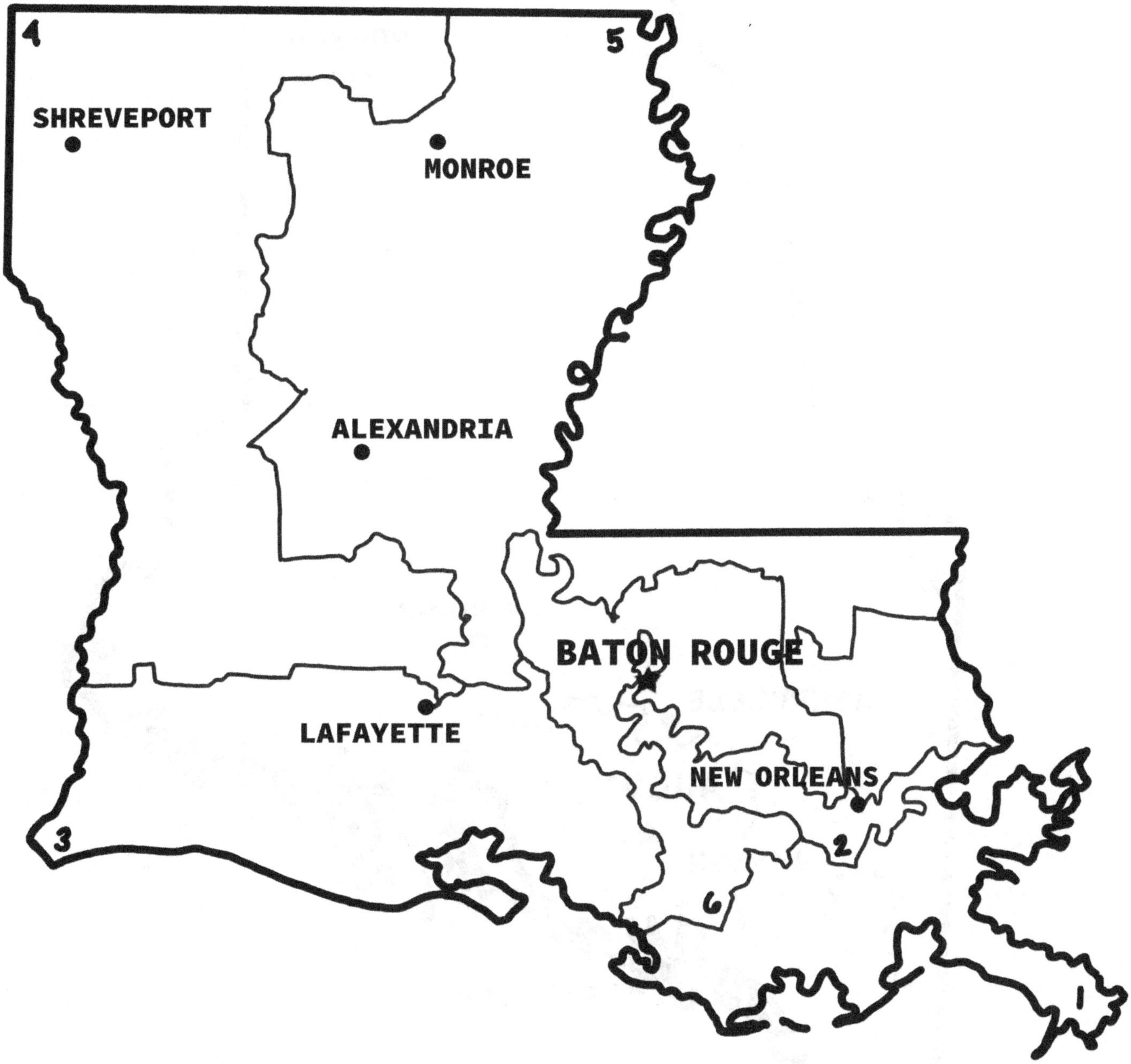

MAINE

Population: 1.3 million
Representatives: 2

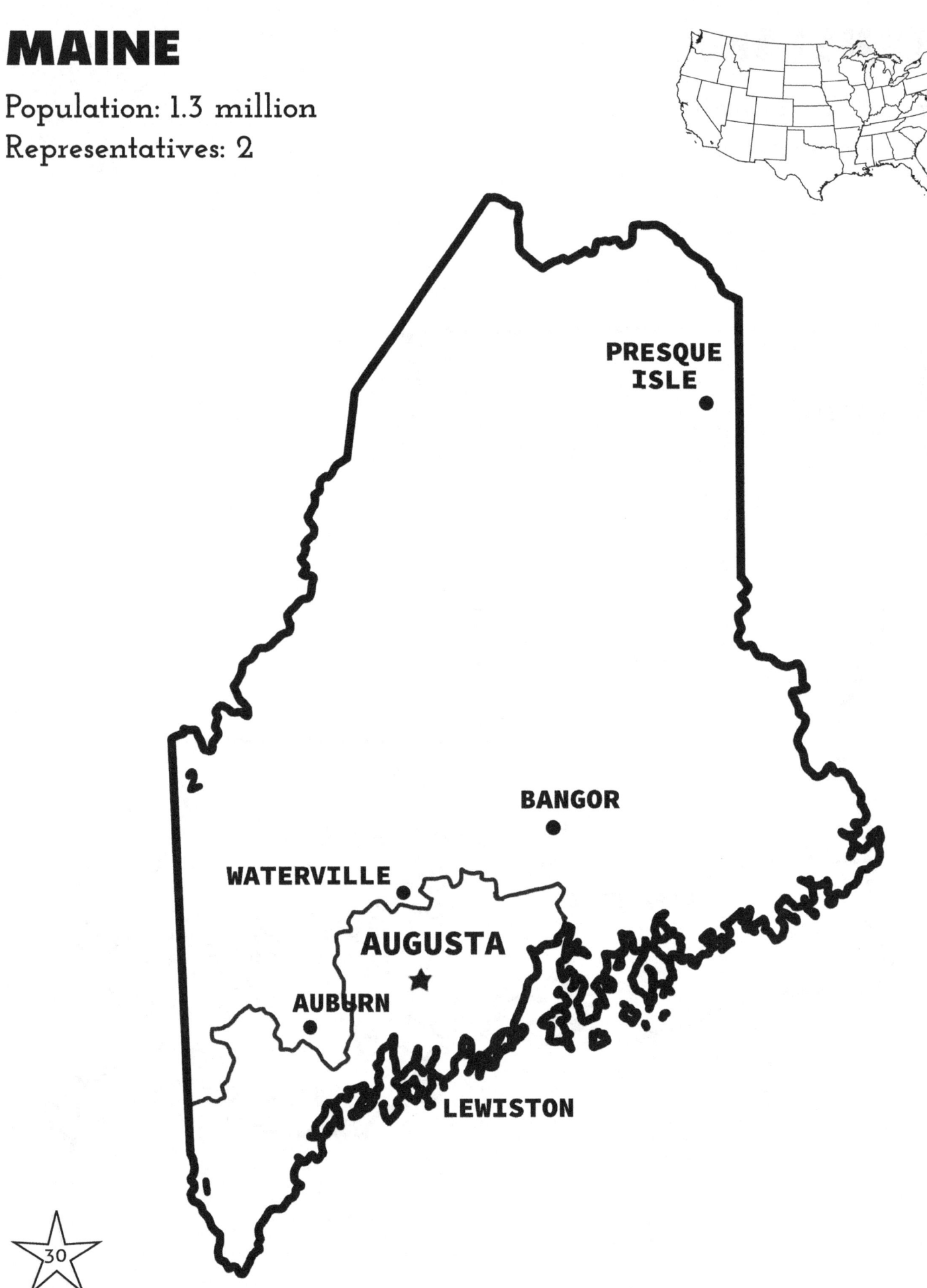

MARYLAND

Population: 6.0 million
Representatives: 8

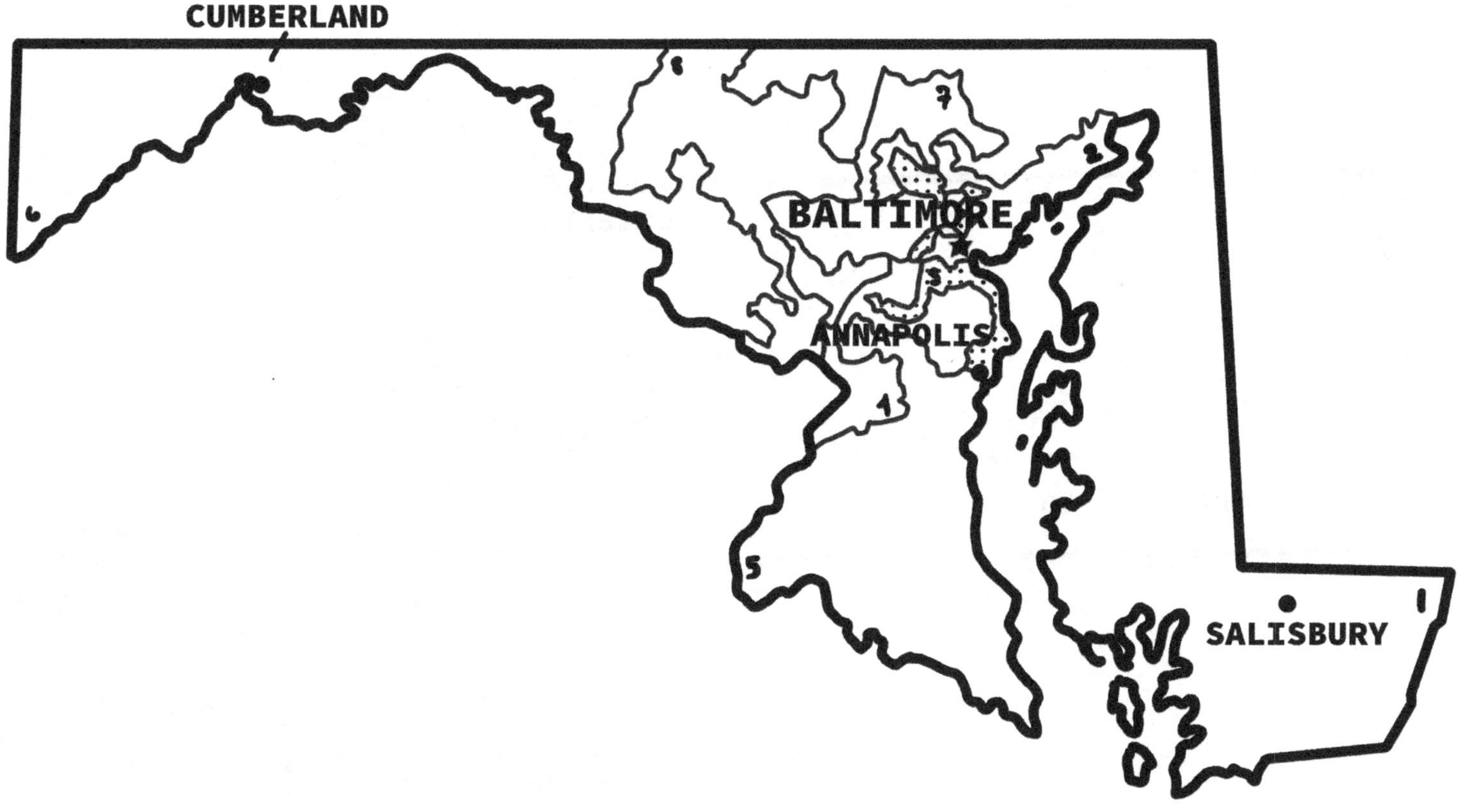

MASSACHUSETTS

Population: 6.7 million
Representatives: 9

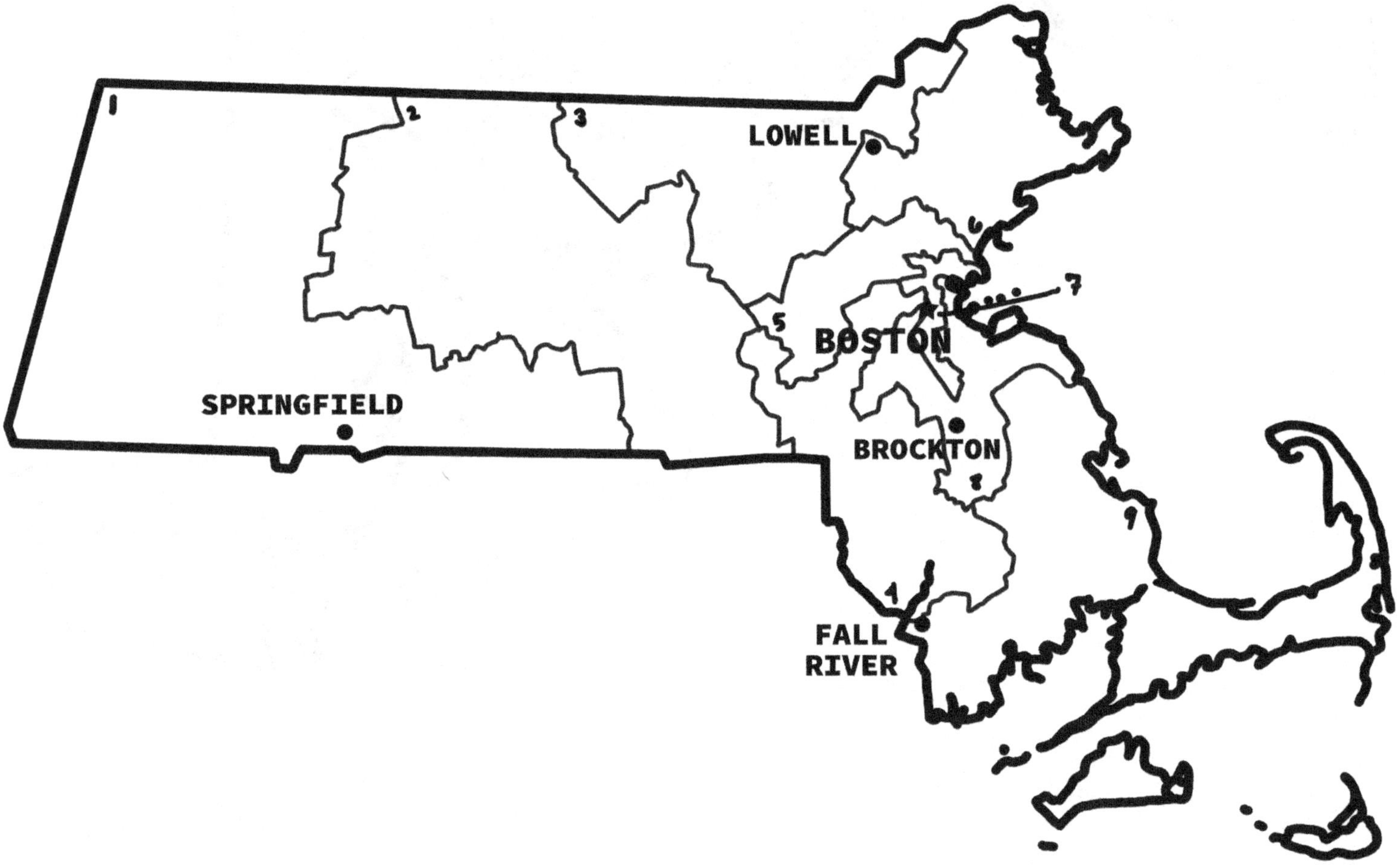

MICHIGAN

Population: 9.9 million
Representatives: 14

33

MINNESOTA

Population: 5.4 million

Representatives: 8

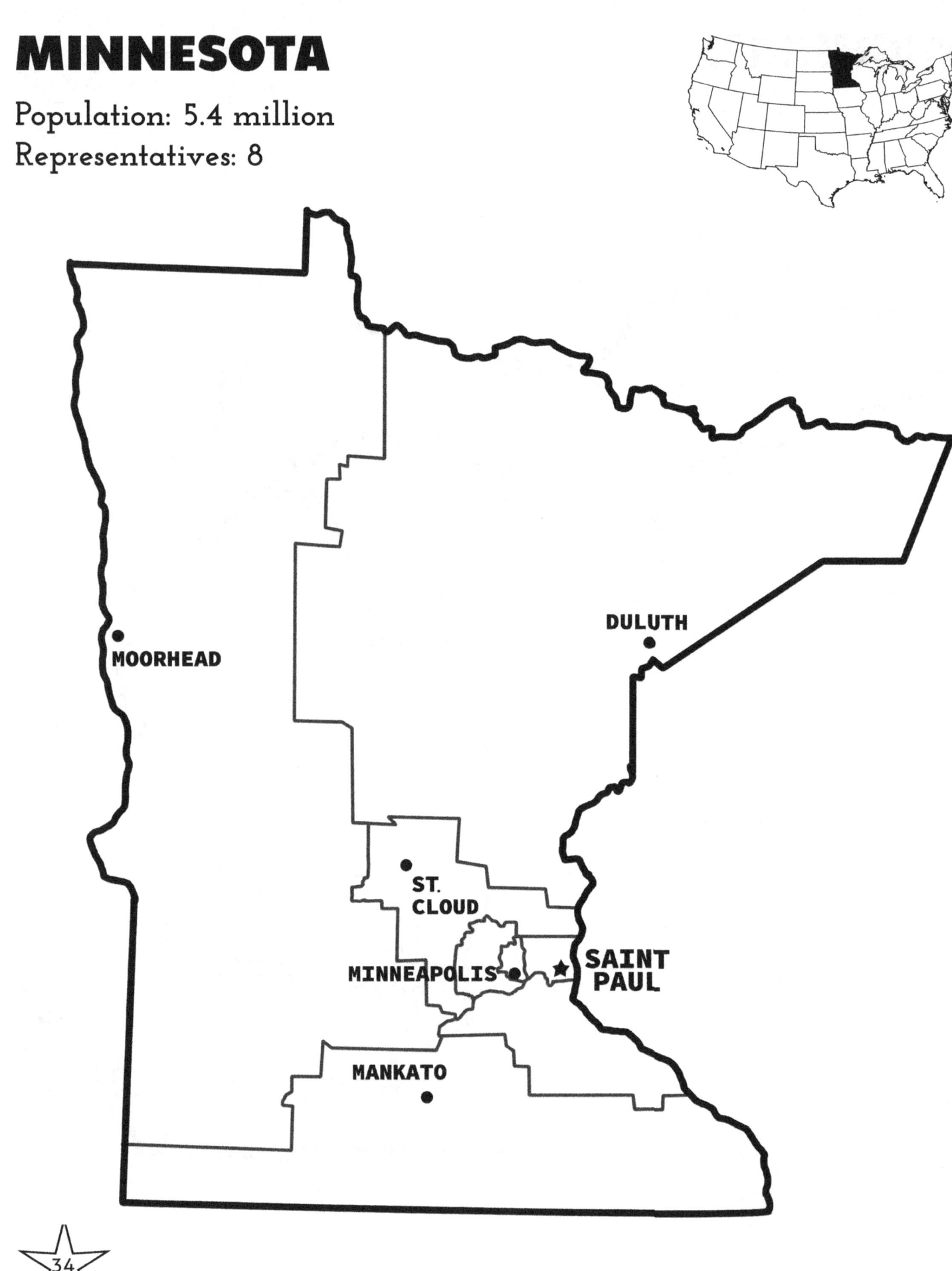

MISSISSIPPI

Population: 2.9 million
Representatives: 4

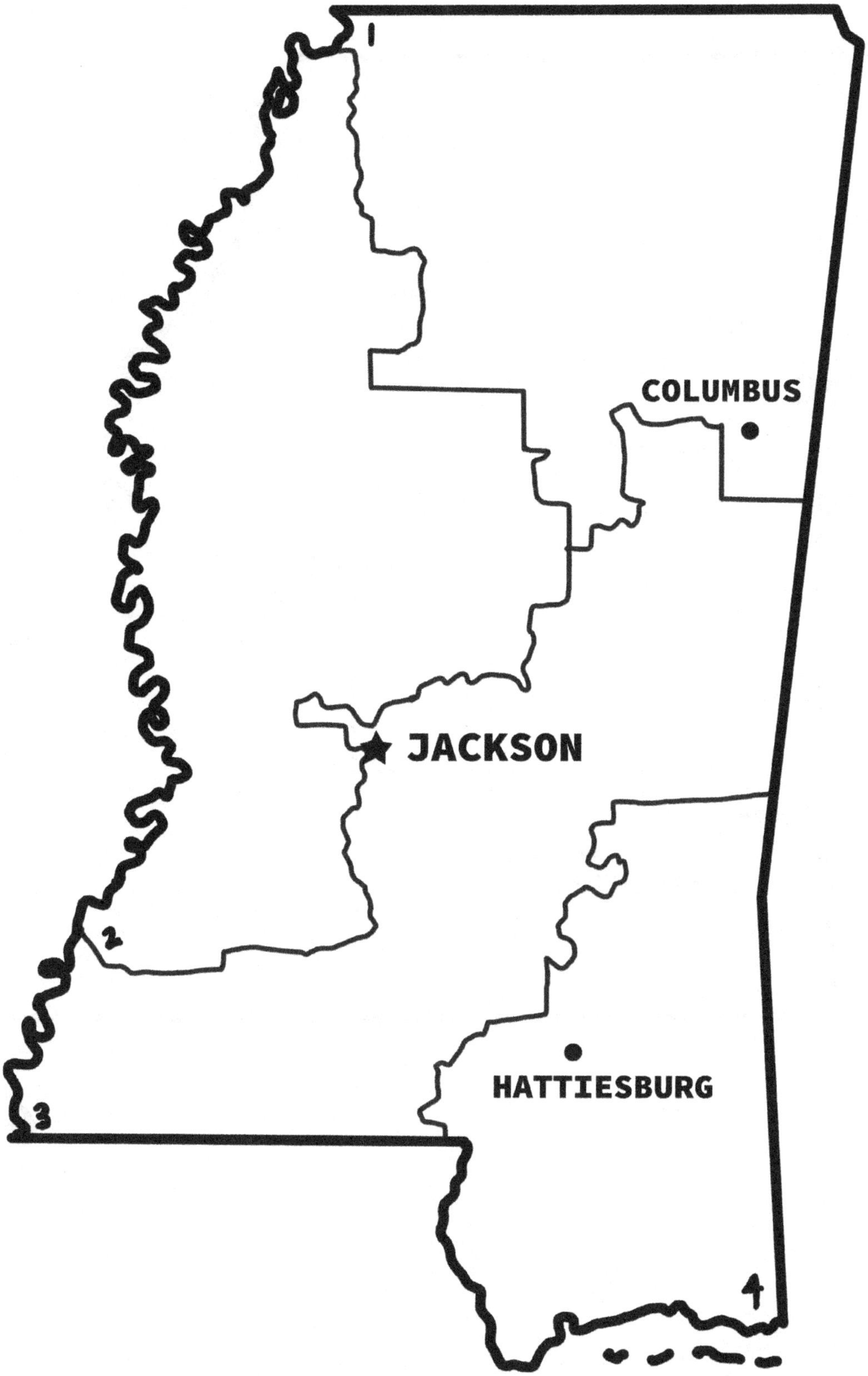

- 1
- COLUMBUS
- ★ JACKSON
- 2
- 3
- HATTIESBURG
- 4

35

MISSOURI

Population: 6.1 million
Representatives: 8

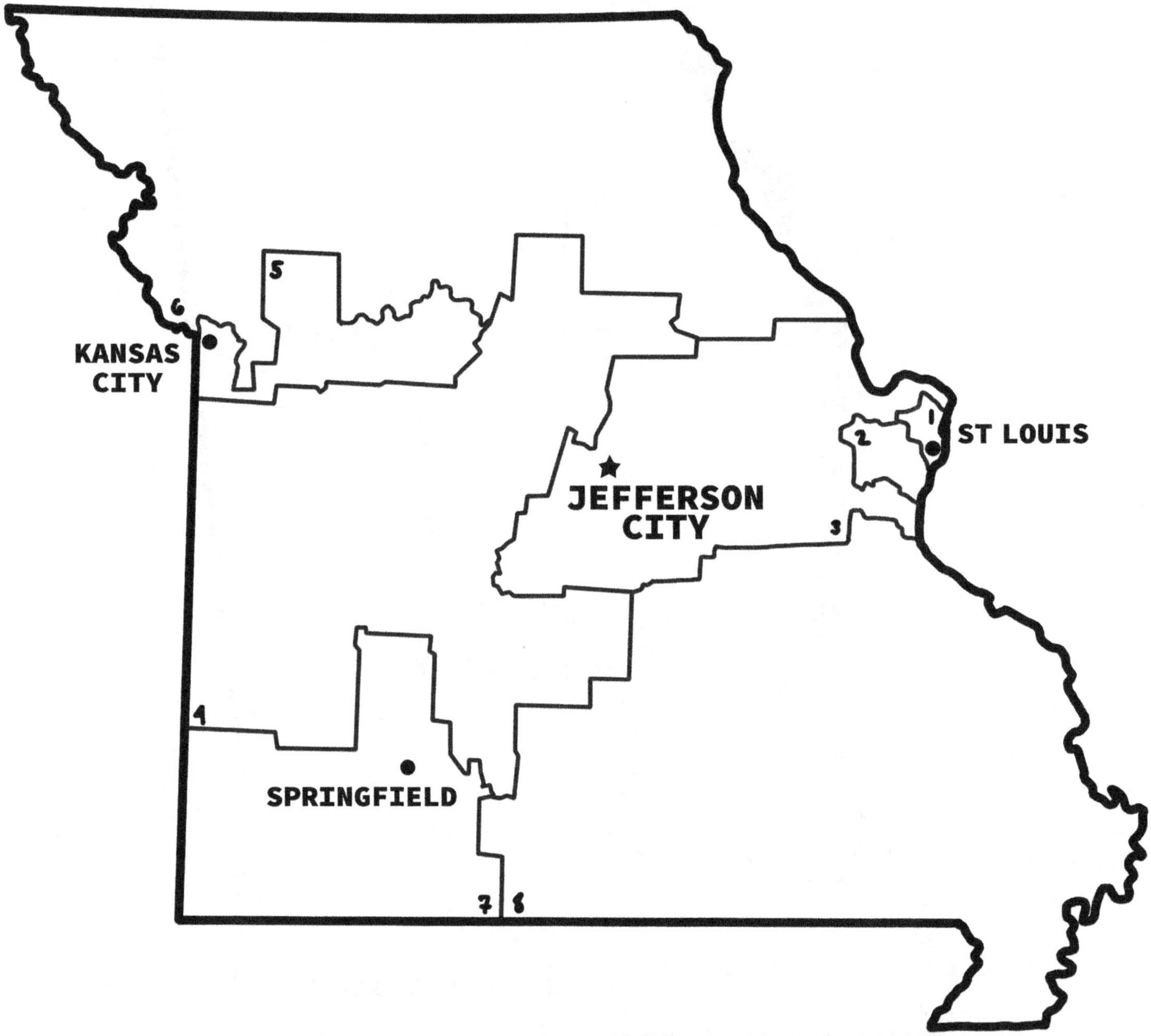

MONTANA

Population: 1.1 million
Representatives: 1

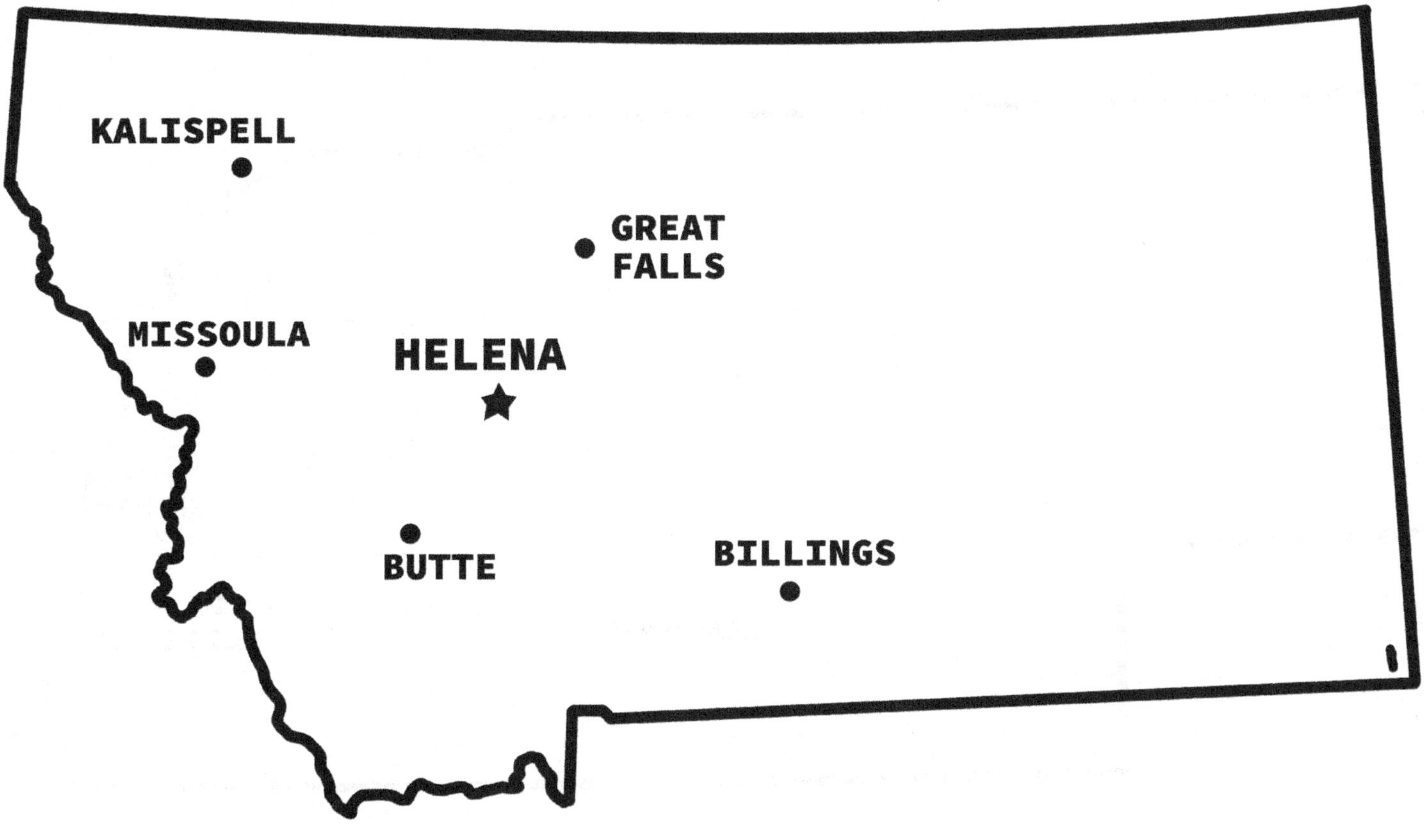

- KALISPELL
- GREAT FALLS
- MISSOULA
- HELENA ★
- BUTTE
- BILLINGS

NEBRASKA

Population: 1.8 million
Representatives: 3

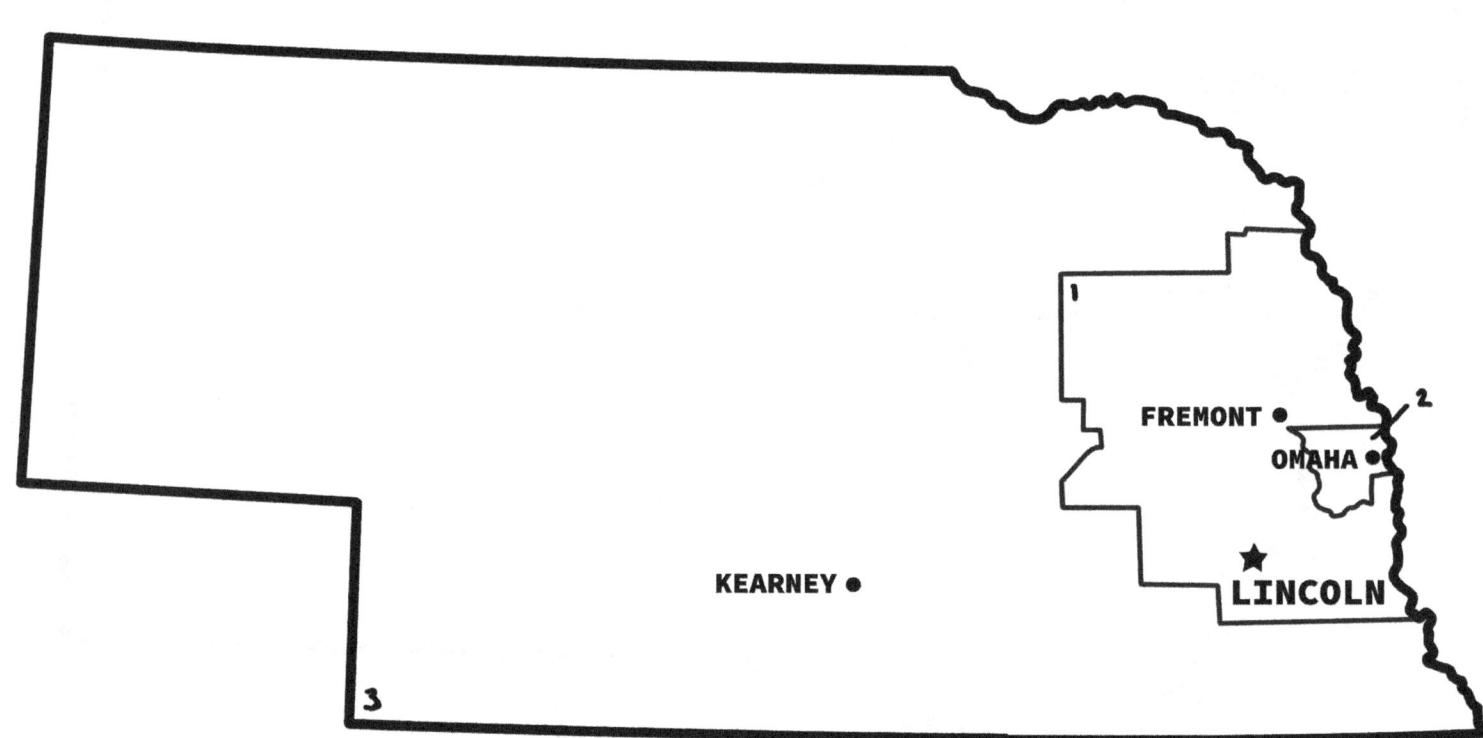

NEVADA

Population: 2.8 million
Representatives: 4

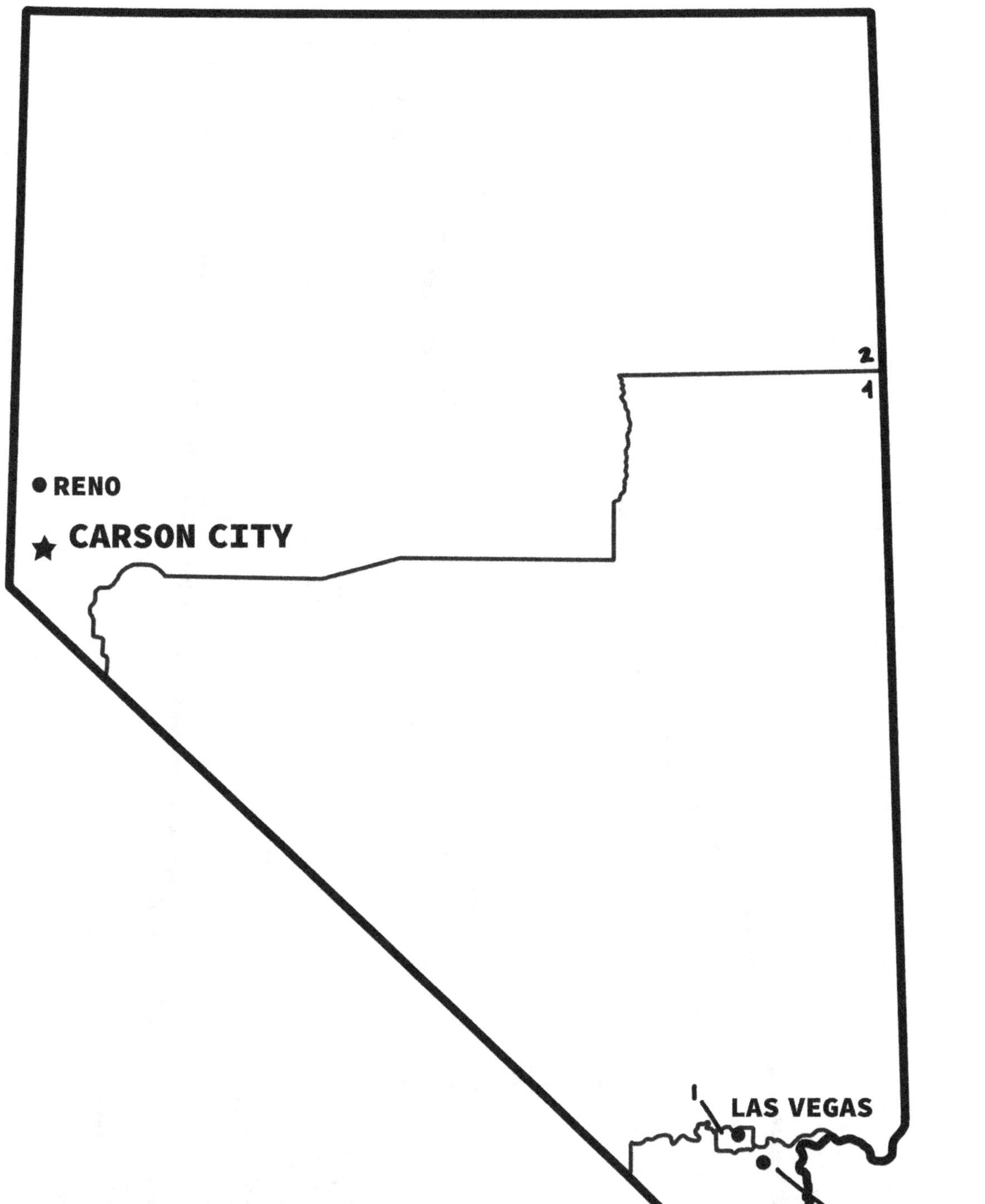

• RENO
★ **CARSON CITY**

1 **LAS VEGAS**
2
4
3
HENDERSON

39

NEW HAMPSHIRE

Population: 1.3 million
Representatives: 2

CONCORD ★

MANCHESTER

NASHUA

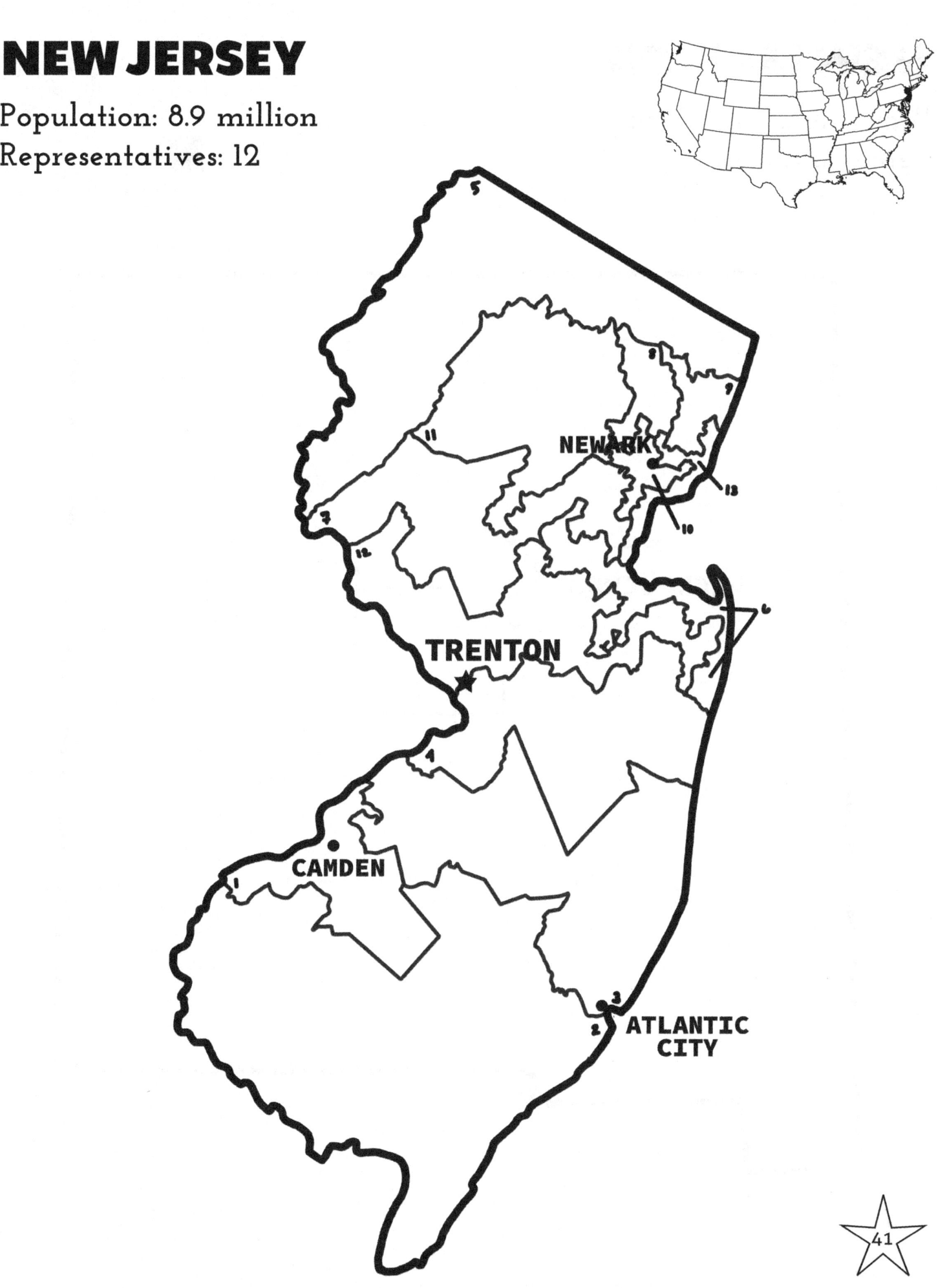

NEW JERSEY

Population: 8.9 million
Representatives: 12

NEW MEXICO

Population: 2.1 million
Representatives: 3

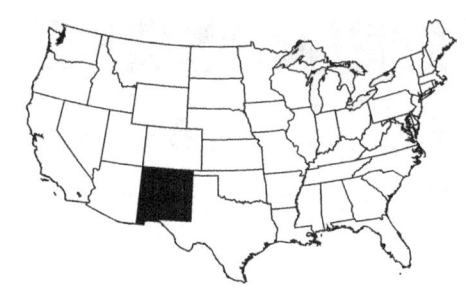

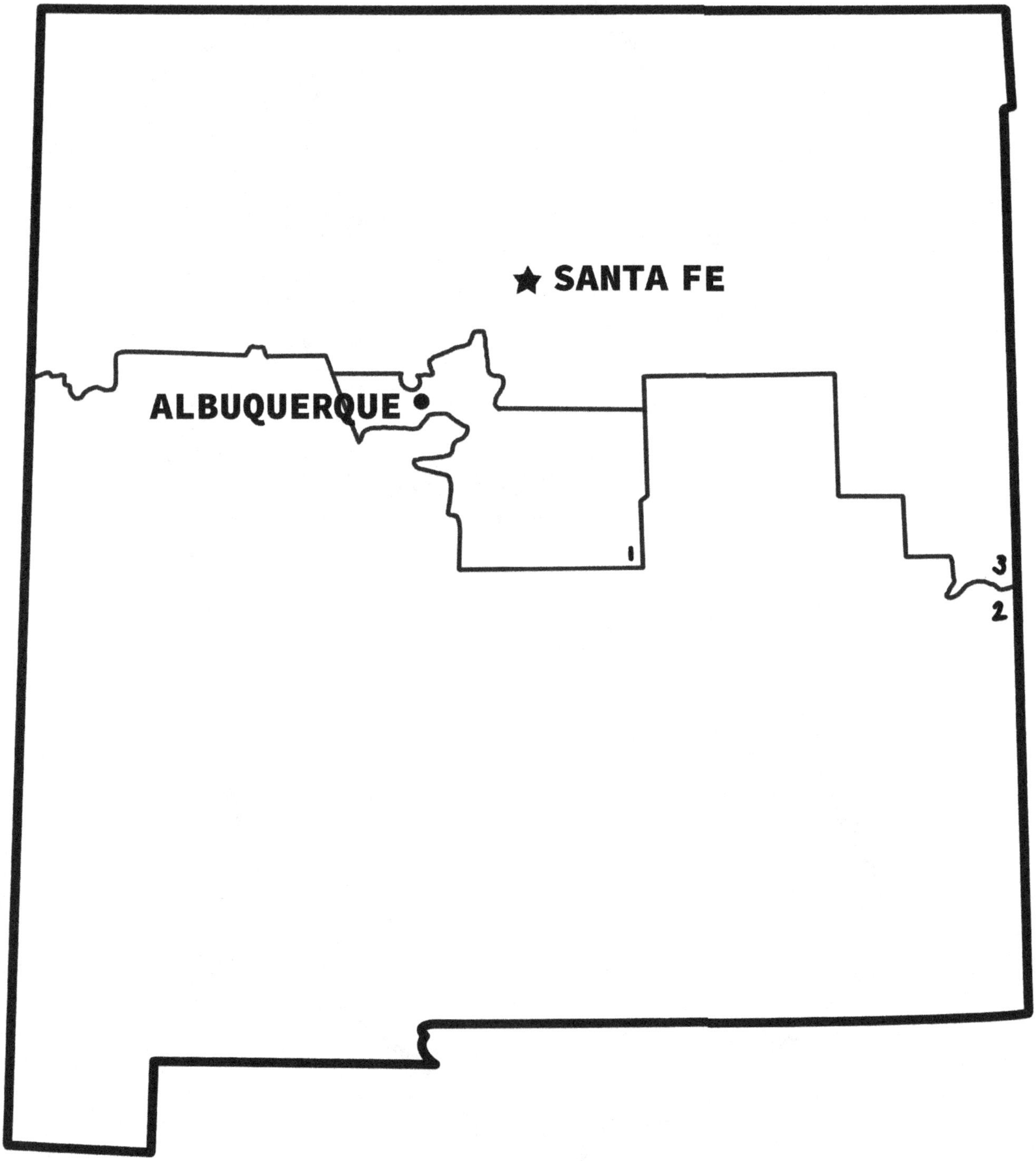

SANTA FE
ALBUQUERQUE
1
3
2

NEW YORK

Population: 8.4 million
Representatives: 27

NORTH CAROLINA

Population: 10.0 million
Representatives: 13

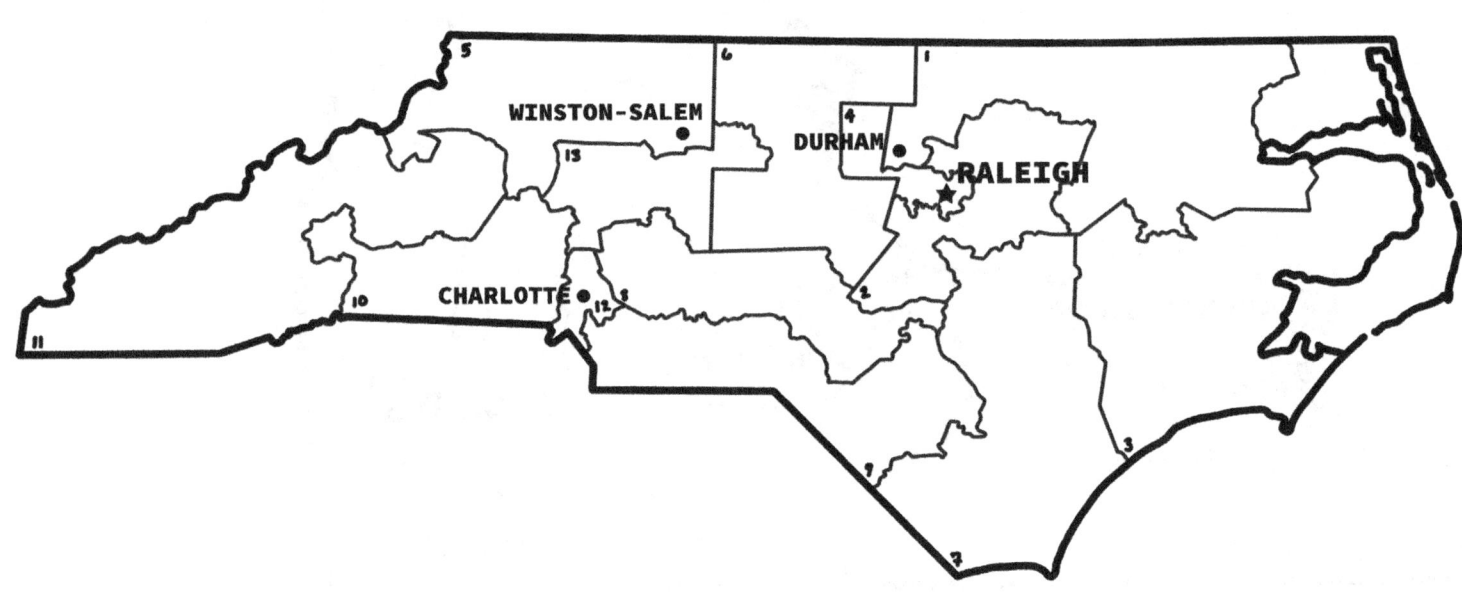

NORTH DAKOTA

Population: 0.8 million
Representatives: 1

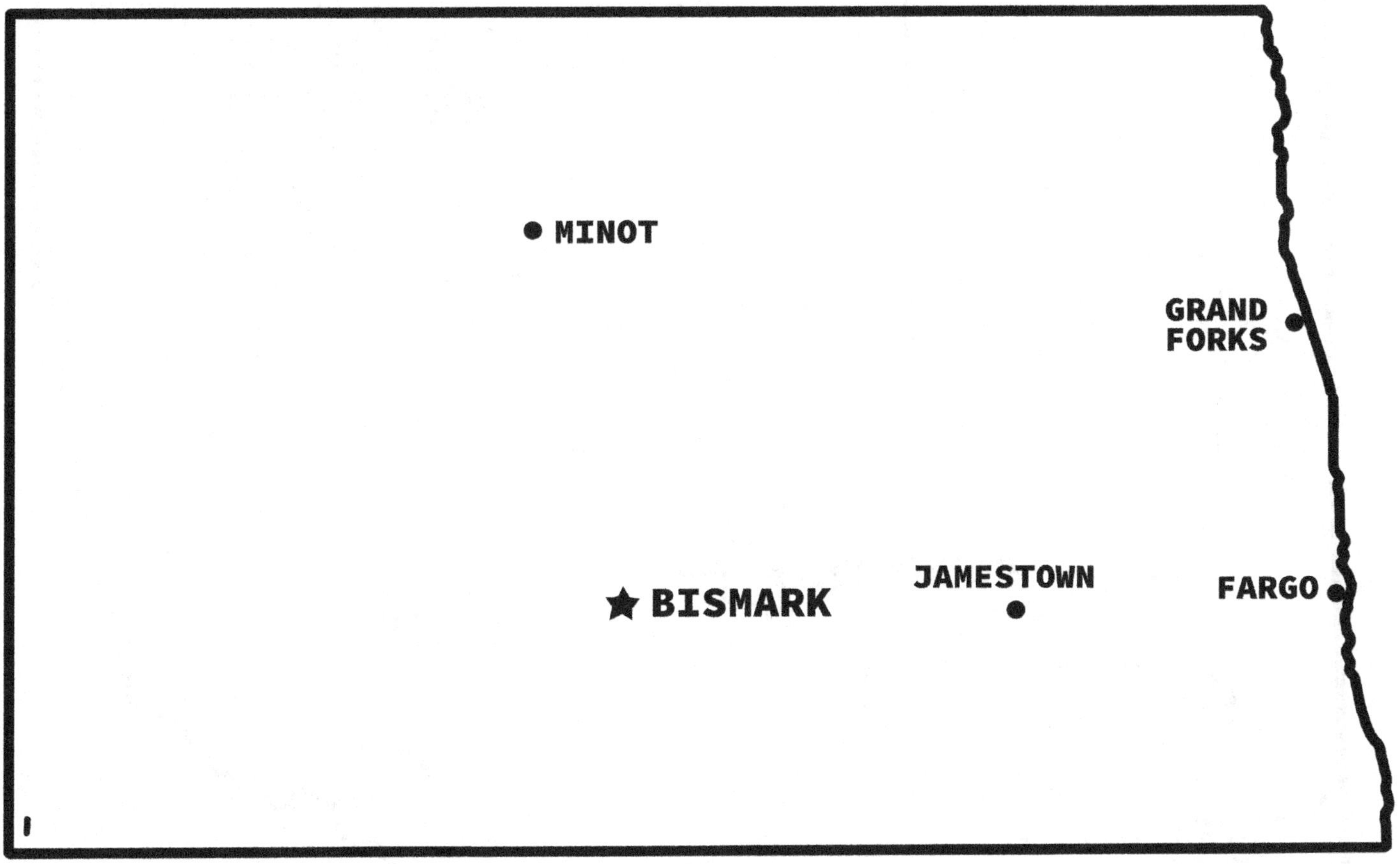

- MINOT
- GRAND FORKS
- ★ BISMARK
- JAMESTOWN
- FARGO

OHIO

Population: 11.6 million
Representatives: 16

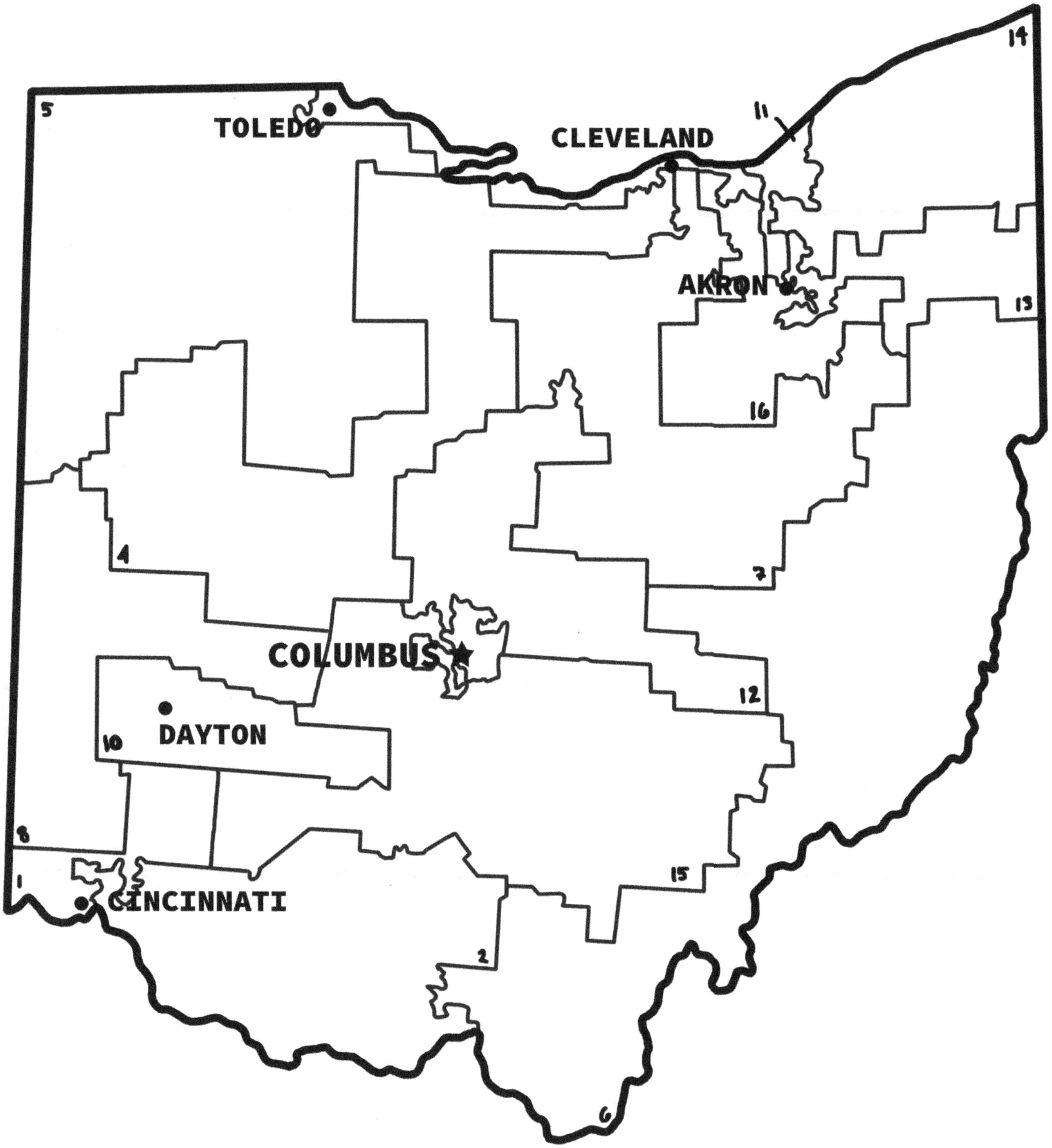

OKLAHOMA

Population: 3.9 million
Representatives: 5

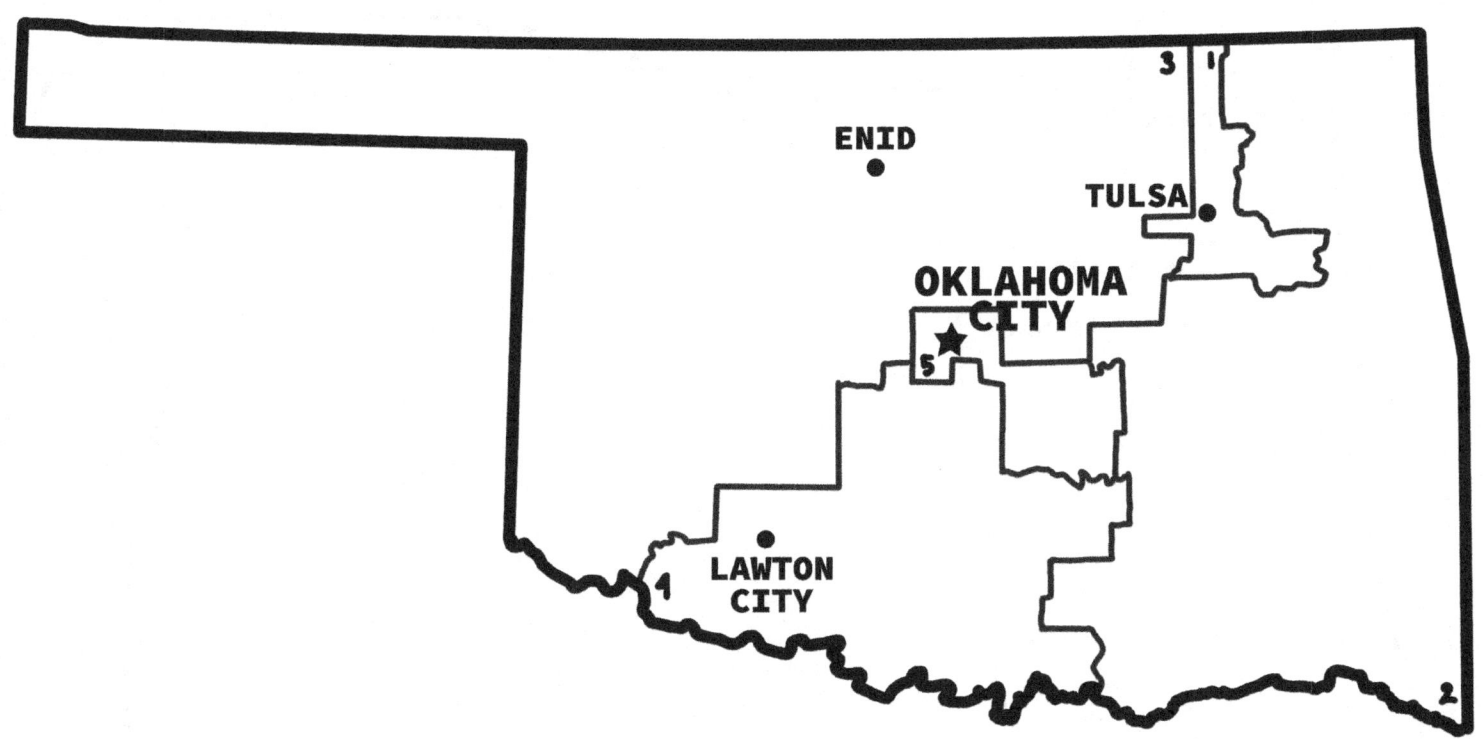

OREGON

Population: 4.0 million
Representatives: 5

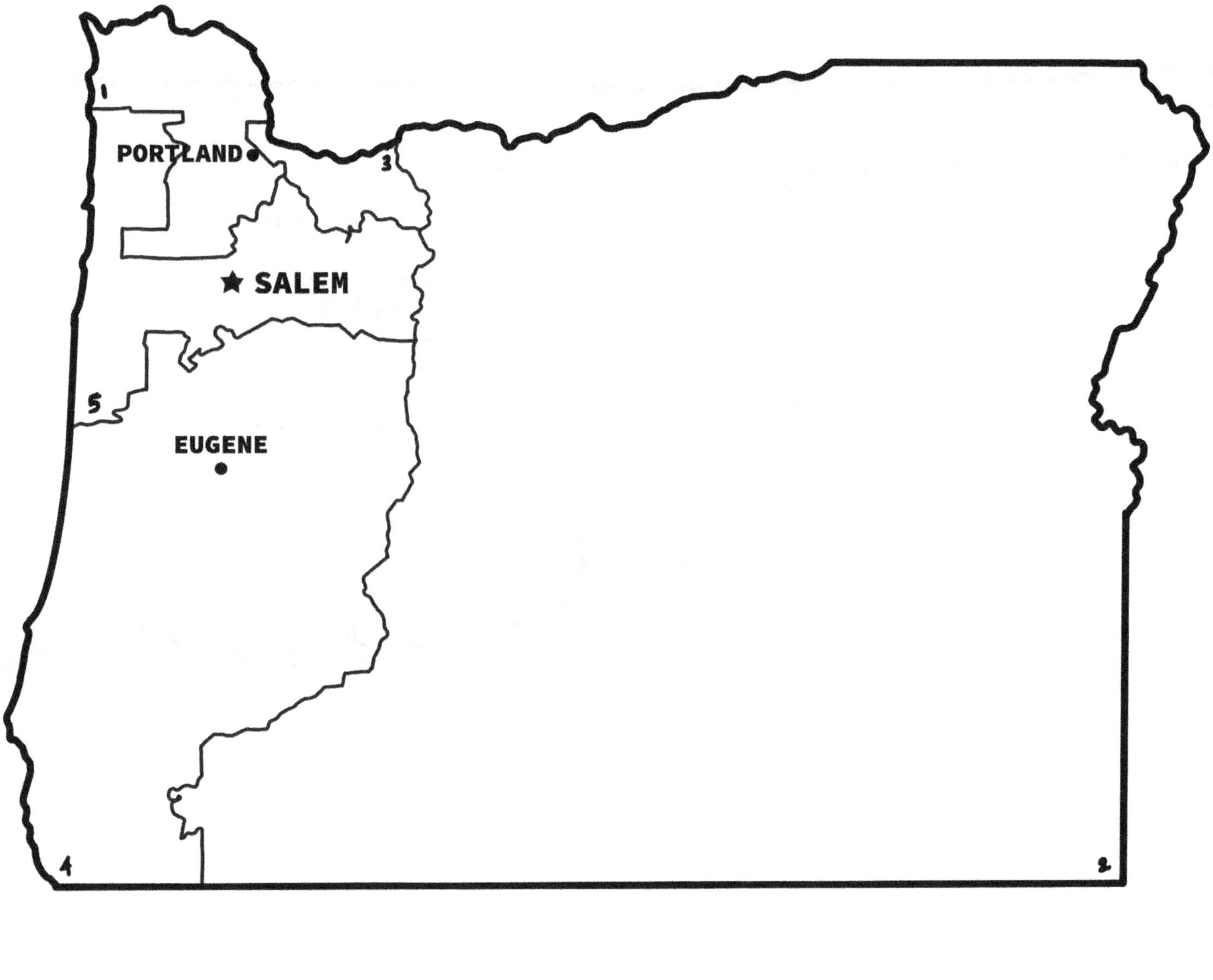

PENNSYLVANIA

Population: 12.8 million
Representatives: 18

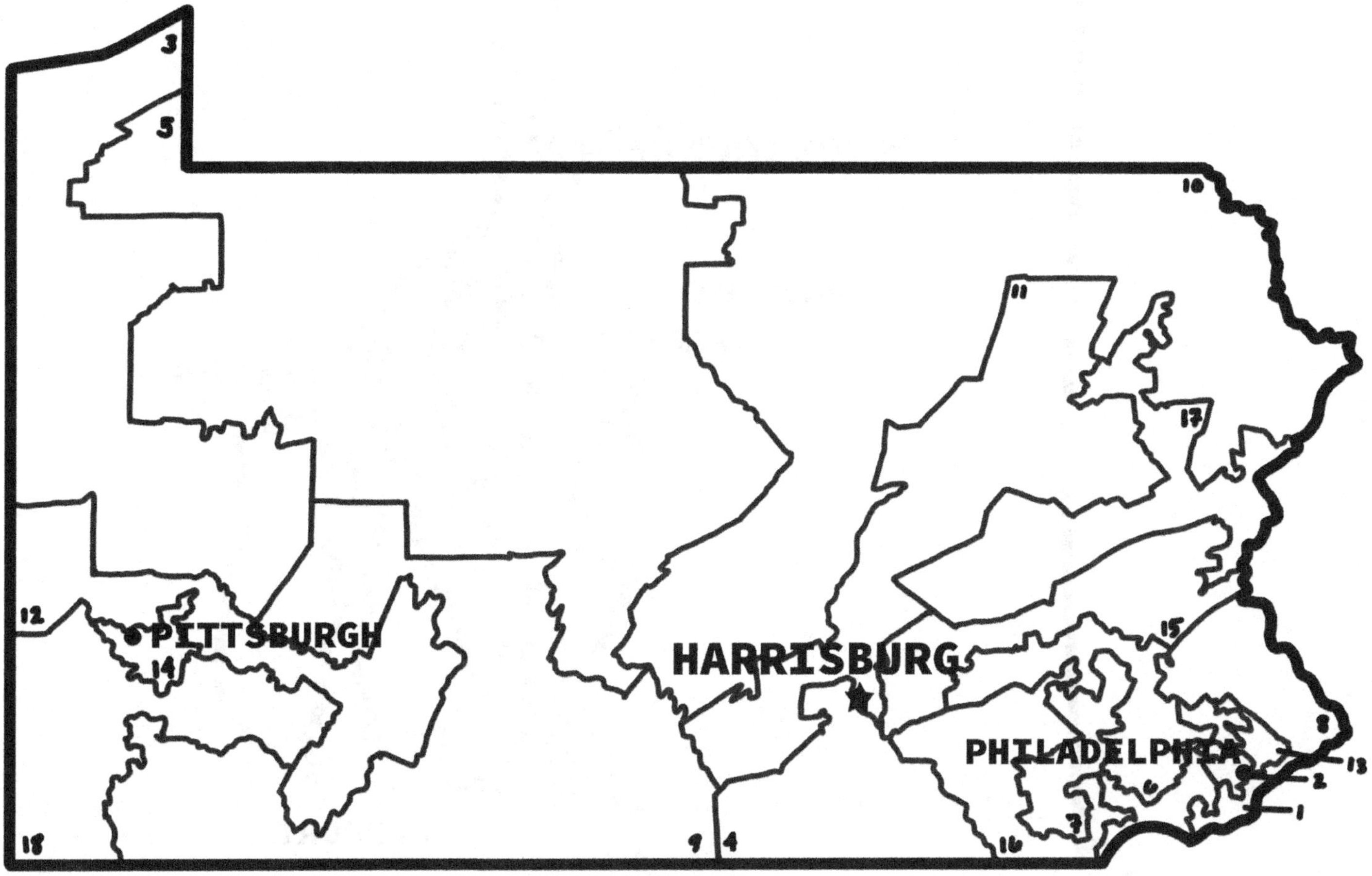

RHODE ISLAND

Population: 1.0 million
Representatives: 2

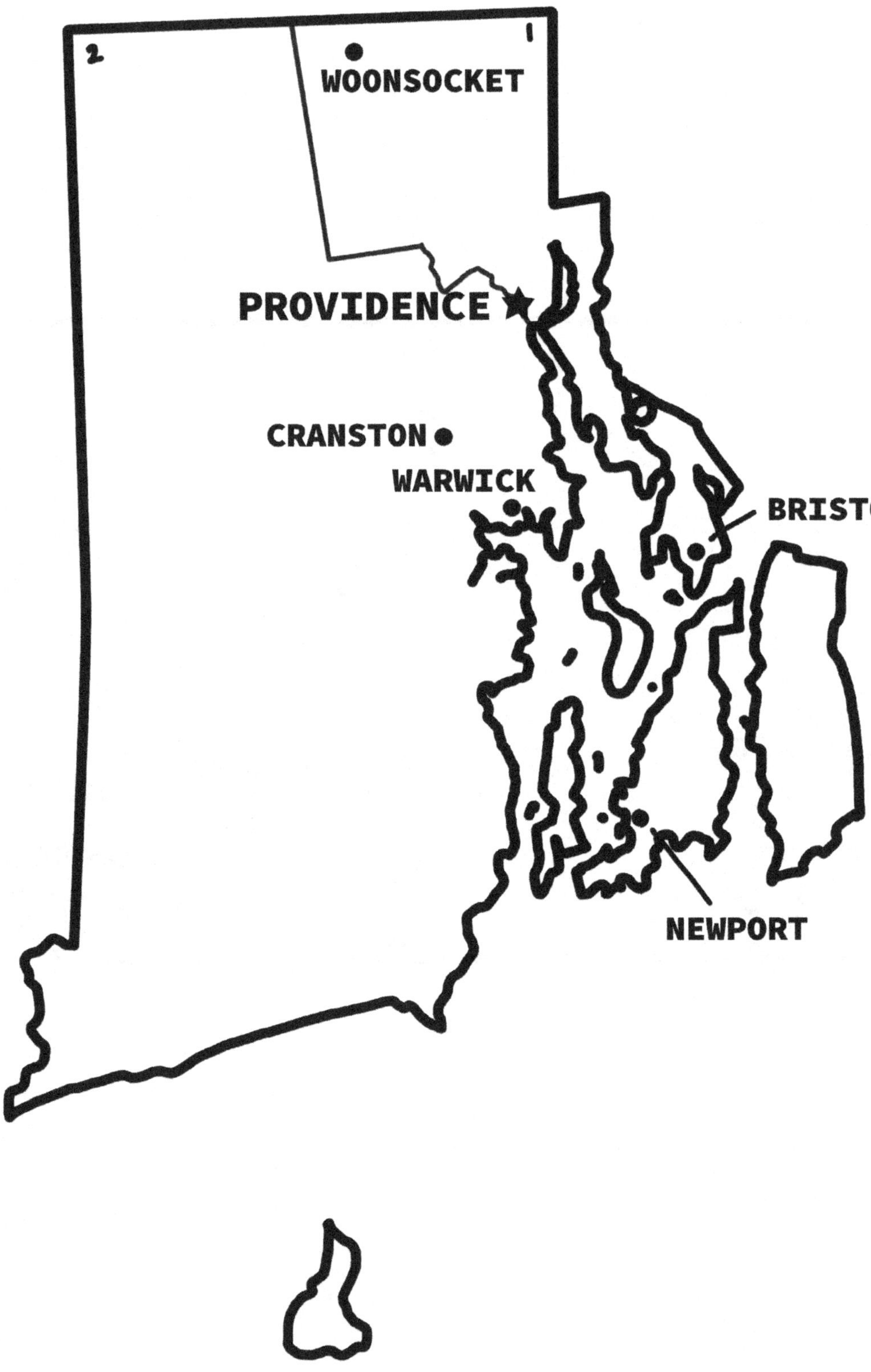

- WOONSOCKET
- PROVIDENCE ★
- CRANSTON
- WARWICK
- BRISTOL
- NEWPORT

SOUTH CAROLINA

Population: 4.8 million
Representatives: 7

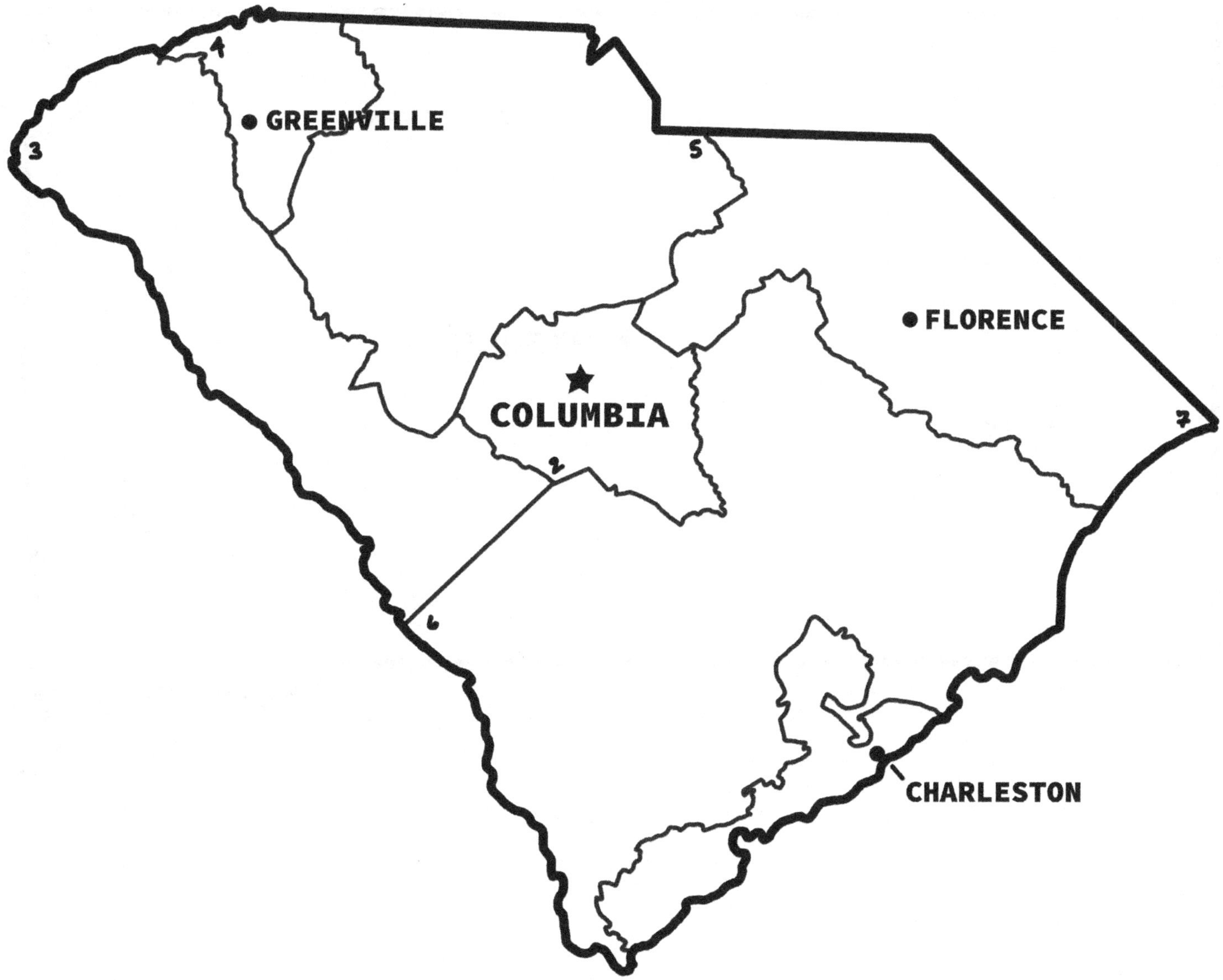

- GREENVILLE
- COLUMBIA ★
- FLORENCE
- CHARLESTON

SOUTH DAKOTA

Population: 0.9 million
Representatives: 1

- ABERDEEN
- ★ PIERRE
- RAPID CITY
- SIOUX FALLS

TENNESSEE

Population: 6.6 million
Representatives: 9

TEXAS

Population: 27.4 million
Representatives: 36

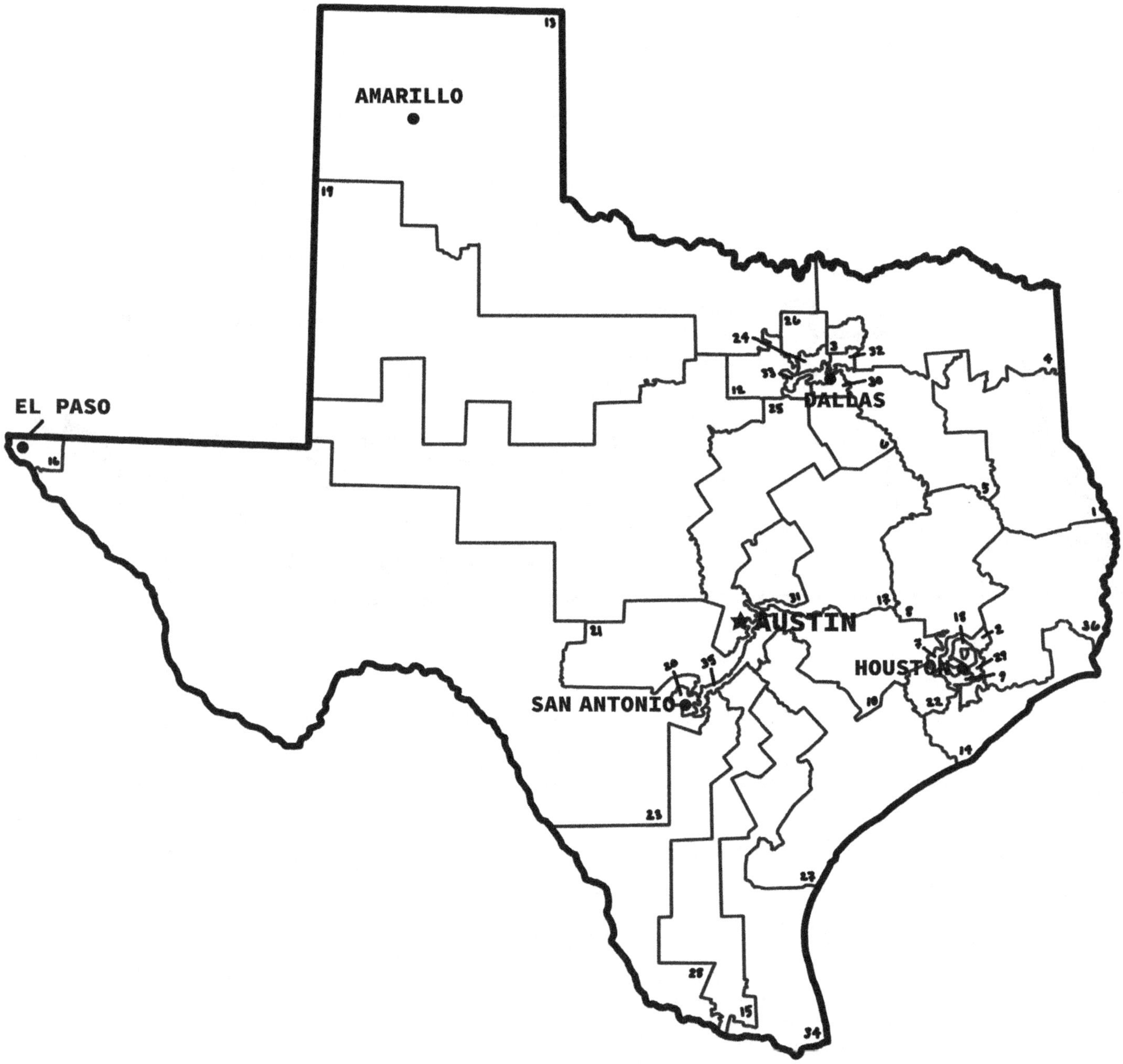

UTAH

Population: 2.9 million
Representatives: 4

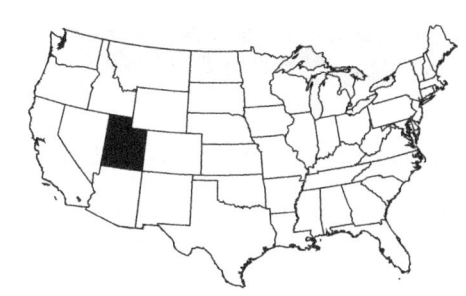

1

● SALT LAKE CITY ★
● WEST VALLEY CITY

● PROVO

4

2 ● ST GEORGE

3

55

VERMONT

Population: 0.6 million
Representatives: 1

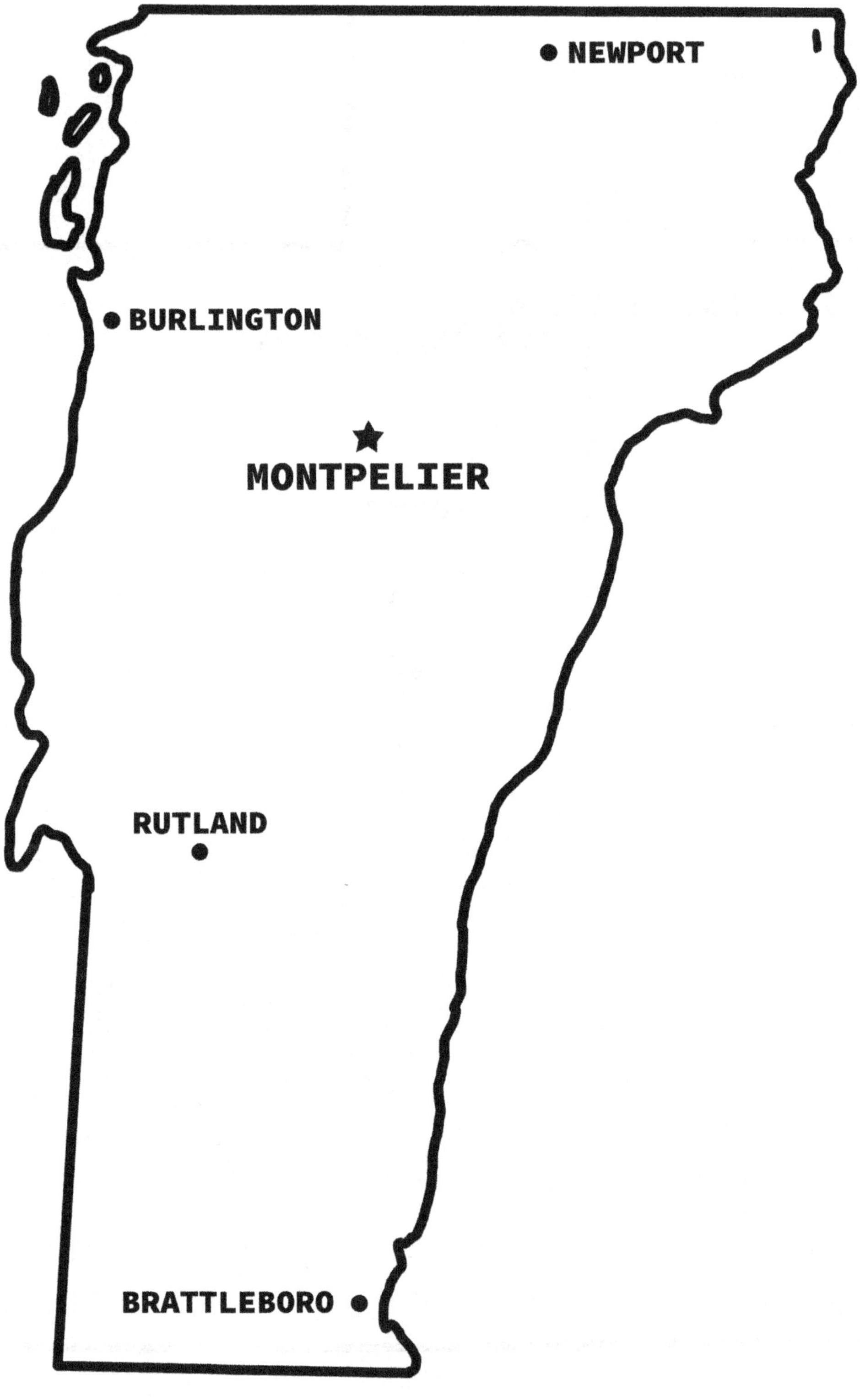

● NEWPORT

● BURLINGTON

★ MONTPELIER

● RUTLAND

● BRATTLEBORO

VIRGINIA

Population: 8.3 million
Representatives: 11

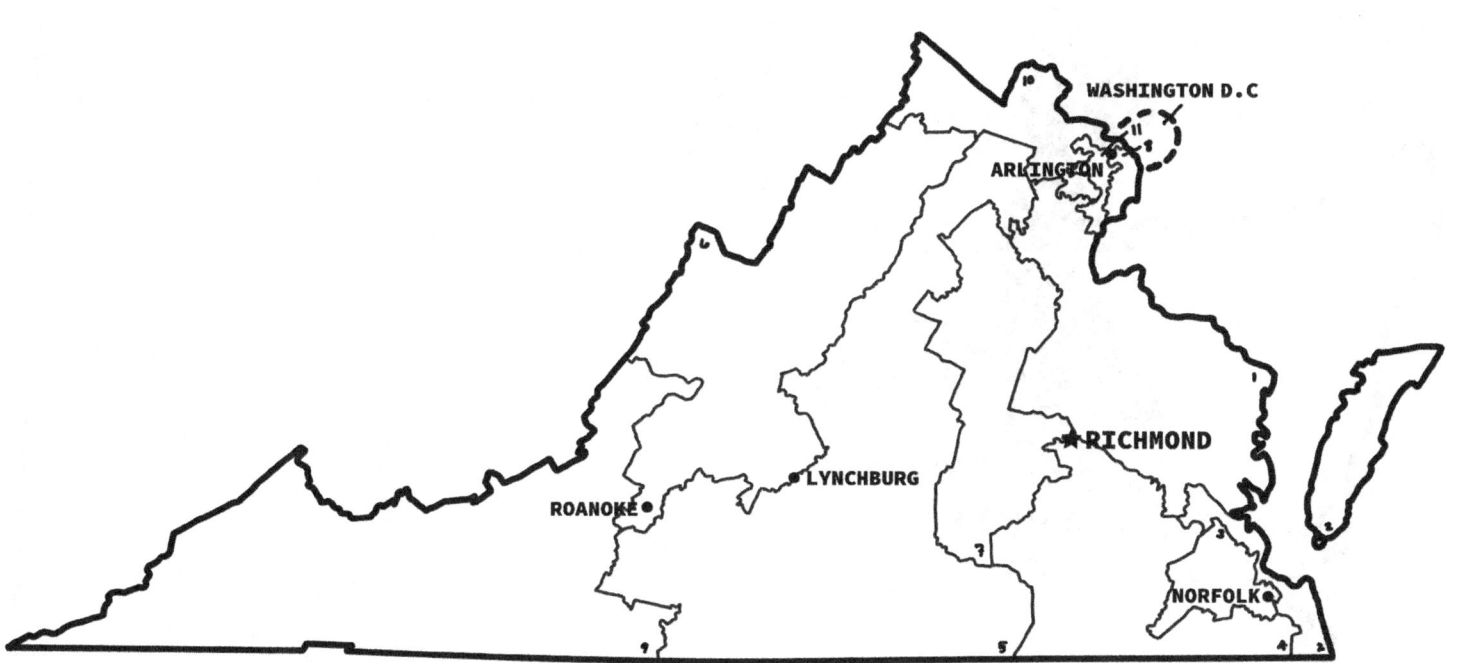

WASHINGTON

Population: 7.1 million
Representatives: 10

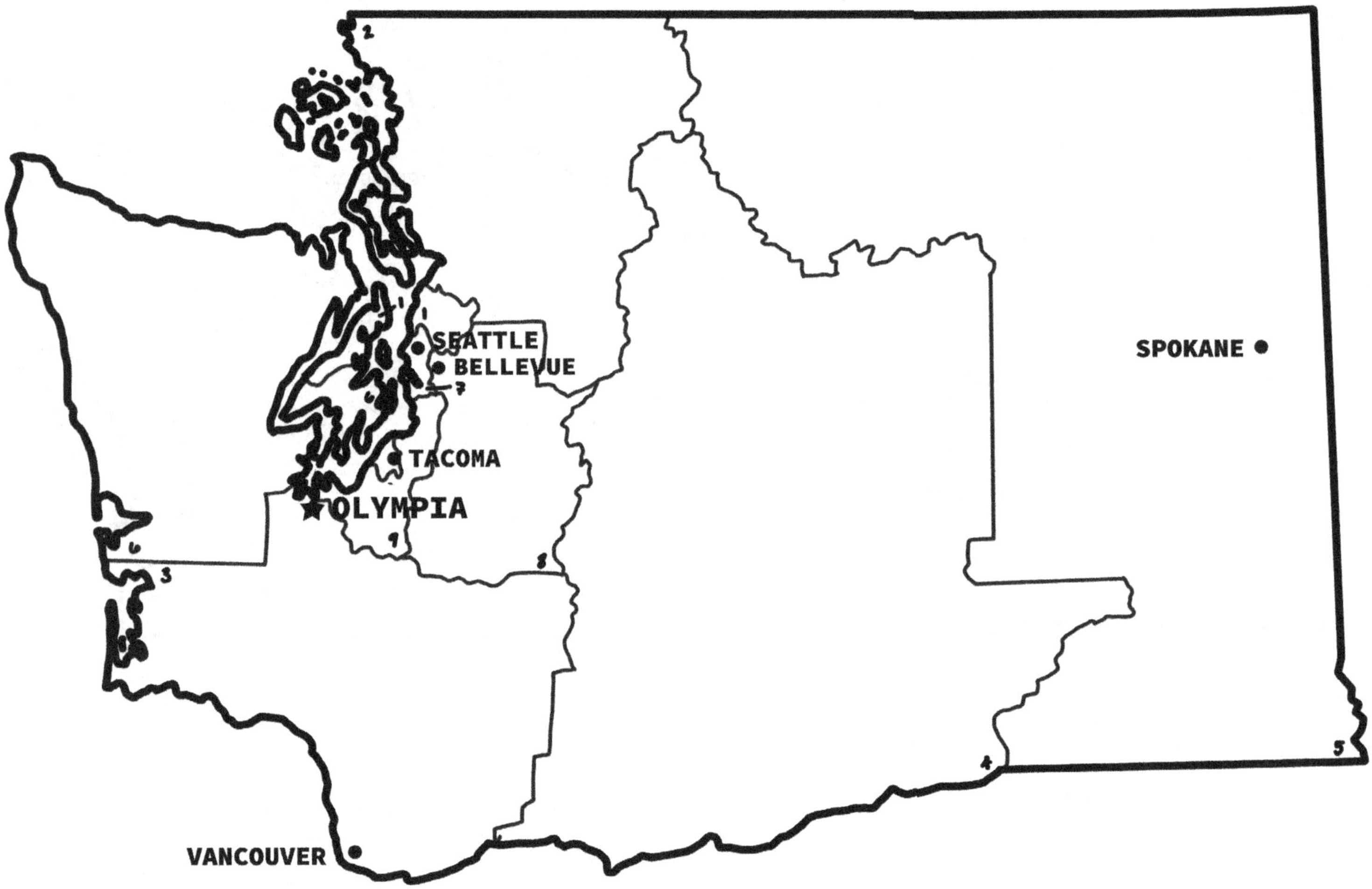

WEST VIRGINIA

Population: 1.8 million
Representatives: 3

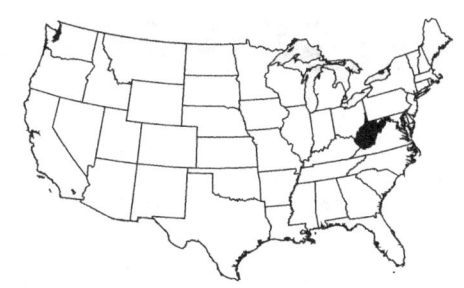

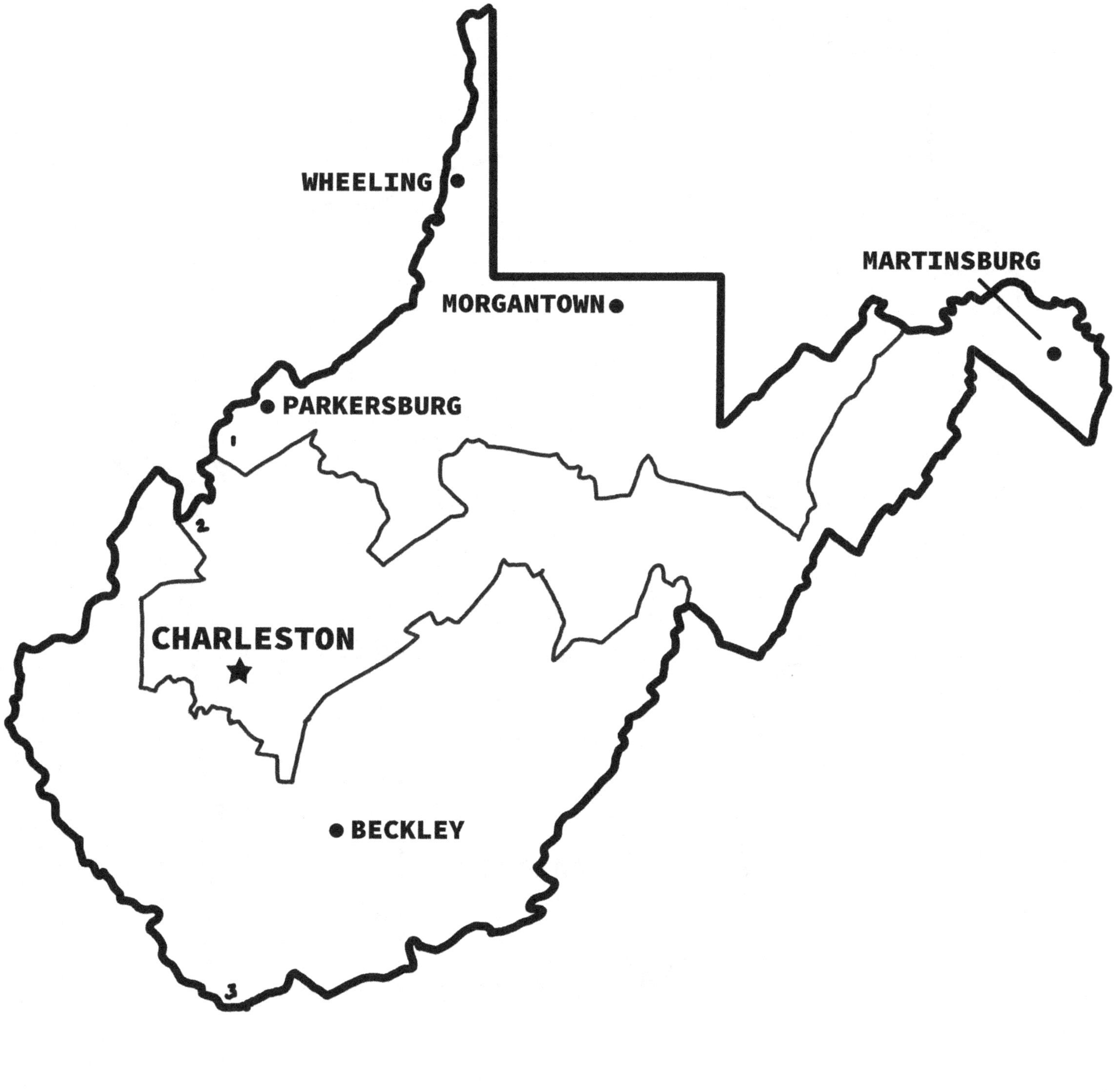
WHEELING
MORGANTOWN
MARTINSBURG
PARKERSBURG
1
2
CHARLESTON
BECKLEY
3

WISCONSIN

Population: 5.7 million
Representatives: 8

WYOMING

Population: 0.6 million
Representatives: 1

- CODY
- CASPER
- ROCK SPRINGS
- CHEYENNE ★

Made in the USA
Monee, IL
28 April 2026